Thoreau and the
Sociological Imagination

Thoreau and the Sociological Imagination

The Wilds of Society

Shawn Chandler Bingham

ROWMAN & LITTLEFIELD PUBLISHERS, INC.
Lanham • Boulder • New York • Toronto • Plymouth, UK

ROWMAN & LITTLEFIELD PUBLISHERS, INC.

Published in the United States of America
by Rowman & Littlefield Publishers, Inc.
A wholly owned subsidiary of The Rowman & Littlefield Publishing Group, Inc.
4501 Forbes Boulevard, Suite 200, Lanham, Maryland 20706
www.rowmanlittlefield.com

Estover Road
Plymouth PL6 7PY
United Kingdom

British Library Cataloguing in Publication Information Available

Library of Congress Cataloging-in-Publication Data

Bingham, Shawn Chandler, 1976–
   Thoreau and the sociological imagination : the wilds of society / Shawn Chandler
Bingham.
     p. cm.
   Includes bibliographical references.
   ISBN-13: 978-0-7425-6058-1 (cloth : alk. paper)
   ISBN-10: 0-7425-6058-9 (cloth : alk. paper)
   ISBN-13: 978-0-7425-6059-8 (pbk. : alk. paper)
   ISBN-10: 0-7425-6059-7 (pbk. : alk. paper)
  1. Thoreau, Henry David, 1817-1862—Political and social views. 2. Social change. 3.
Sociology—Methodology. 4. United States—Social conditions. I. Title.
   HM831.B558 2008
   301.092—dc22

                  2007028255

Printed in the United States of America

♾ᵀᴹ The paper used in this publication meets the minimum requirements of
American National Standard for Information Sciences—Permanence of Paper
for Printed Library Materials, ANSI/NISO Z39.48-1992.

For Angela and Eva Grace,
For the rest of my very wonderful and very bizarre family,
And in memory of my "Authors" partner, Ivaloo

Wherever men have lived there is a story to be told, and it depends chiefly on the storyteller or historian whether that is interesting or not. You are simply a witness on the stand to tell what you know about your neighbors and your neighborhood.

All this is perfectly distinct to an observant eye, and yet could easily go unnoticed by most.

—Henry David Thoreau, March 18 and November 3, 1861

The best you can write will be the best you are. Every sentence is the result of a long probation. The author's character is read from title-page to end. Of this he never corrects the proofs.

—Henry David Thoreau, February 28, 1841

How many a man has dated a new era in his life from the reading of a book.

—Henry David Thoreau, *Walden*

O how I laugh when I think of my vague indefinite riches. No run on my bank can drain it, for my wealth is not possession but enjoyment. If the day and the night are such that you greet them with joy and life emits a fragrance like flowers and sweet-scented herbs-is more elastic, starry, and immortal-that is your success.

—Henry David Thoreau, letter to Harrison Blake, 1856

~

Contents

~

Preface

In the fall of 2001, while roaming through a bookstore in Bowie, Maryland, I came across Henry David Thoreau's *Walden* on the sale rack, and decided to pick it up. I had read the book years before, but in that instant saw it as an escape from the "turgid and polysyllabic prose" of the sociological writing I was poring through as a graduate student.[1] I was immediately surprised by the breadth of topics Thoreau addressed that are core concerns of modern sociology—class, poverty, race, work and leisure, progress, world commerce, government, the individual and society, and social forces.

Over the course of reading more about this American thinker, I discovered that Thoreau's ideas have been used by a wide range of academic disciplines, including philosophy, political science, economics, environmental studies, and American literature. Yet, as a result of a more insular approach to social theory, my own discipline—sociology—has been silent about thinkers such as Henry David Thoreau. Even though his writings strike at the heart of socio-structural issues, and despite the fact that his influence can be traced to several modern social reform movements, I was surprised to find that there had been no systematic exploration of Thoreau's writings from a sociological perspective.

My objective in writing this book was threefold. First, and foremost, I wanted to demonstrate that while sociology was in its infancy in Europe, and the social science movement was just being conceived in the United States, Henry David Thoreau was engaging in sociological thought and analysis in his own uniquely American way. His examination of social structures, such as the economy, his deconstruction of "progress," and his analysis of social change reflect a steady practice of the "sociological imagination" at a time when this way of thinking was in its formative stages. While I do make the case that Thoreau possessed sociological consciousness, however, *I do not argue that he was a sociologist.* This is an important distinction because many of the individuals who had a place in the development of social theory were themselves not sociologists. Secondly, I wanted to echo the voice of others who have sounded warnings of the dangers of holding tightly to a rigid view of the discipline of sociology. I am hoping to build on the tradition of C. Wright Mills, Peter Berger, George Ritzer, Patrick McGuire, Patricia Lengermann, and Jill Niebrugge-Brantley, who have all called on sociology to engage in disciplinary self-reflection and critique. Representing social reality is not sociology's exclusive birthright, and this book is an effort to help communicate this idea to others within my field. Indeed, we can learn much from an intellectual like Thoreau, who was, all at once, a poet, writer, social critic, and scientist. He has much to teach us about approaching social inquiry as a craft, rather than a technical or mechanical act. In spirit, then, this book is a caveat that examines Thoreau as one figure among the many whose ideas have not been plumbed by sociology. Finally, to those from other disciplines who already read and enjoy Thoreau's work, I wanted to help provide yet another perspective for examining his writings, proving again that Thoreau was a unique interdisciplinary intellectual who was boundless not only as a hiker, but also as a thinker.

Notes

1. In his work *The Sociological Imagination* (New York: Oxford University Press, 1959), 217, C. Wright Mills uses this phrase to describe the inability of many sociologists to communicate effectively through writing.

~

Acknowledgments

As a student of sociology, I have been taught to recognize the part that biography and environment play in determining "life chances." The following have played a crucial role in my development and thought process during the writing of this book: the Bingham, Black, Maloney, Moss, and Tkacik families; my colleagues at Howard Community College, the University of South Florida, and Saint Leo University; and my dissertation committee at American University. I am also grateful to the editors and staff at Rowman & Littlefield for their progressive willingness to entertain an unorthodox project such as this book. Finally, I owe a great deal to Angela, who endured more than anyone could ever ask: cold dinners, canceled movie nights, books strewn all over our antique furniture, the task of hauling overdue library books to the library at her school because I had reached the limit on my library card, and the stigma of having to tell people at the park that our dog is named "Walden." Thank you.

Chronology

1848	Thoreau presents lecture to Concord Lyceum titled "The Individual in Relation to the State," which later becomes *Resistance to Civil Government*
	The U.S. war with Mexico ends
	Karl Marx's *Communist Manifesto* is published
1849	Thoreau's *A Week on the Concord and Merrimack*, and *Resistance to Civil Government (Civil Disobedience)* are published
	Marx's *Wage Labor and Capital* is published
1851	Spencer's *Social Statics* is published
1852	*Uncle Tom's Cabin*, by Harriet Beecher Stowe, is published
1853	Martineau translates Comte's *Positive Philosophy*; these translations begin to appear in the United States
1854	Thoreau presents "Slavery in Massachusetts" at abolitionist meeting in Framingham, Massachusetts (July)
	Walden; or life in the woods is published by Ticknor and Fields
1857	Thoreau meets Captain John Brown
	The Dred Scott case is heard by Supreme Court
	Thorsten Veblen is born in Cato, Wisconsin (July 30)
	Auguste Comte dies
1858	Emile Durkheim is born in Lorraine, France (April 15)
1859	Thoreau becomes head of the family business
	The first edition of *Walden* sells out
	John Brown leads the raid on a federal arsenal at Harper's Ferry, West Virginia. In response, Thoreau delivers lecture titled "A Plea for Captain John Brown"
	Darwin's *Origin of Species* is published
1860	Thoreau catches a cold while conducting a natural experiment, which leads to an ongoing illness
	Jane Addams is born in Cedarville, Illinois (September 6)
1861	The Civil War begins
1862	Thoreau dies of tuberculosis (May 6)
1863	*Life without Principle* and *Excursions* are published
	President Lincoln signs the Emancipation Proclamation
	George Herbert Mead is born in South Hadley, Massachusetts (February 27)
1864	*The Maine Woods* is published
	Max Weber is born in Thuringia, Germany (April 21)
1865	*Cape Cod* is published
	The Civil War ends
	The American Social Science Association is founded
1866	*A Yankee in Canada, with Anti-Slavery and Reform Papers* is published
1867	Karl Marx's *Das Kapital* (Vol. I) is published

1868	W. E. B. du Bois is born in Great Barrington, Massachusetts (February 23)
1873	Ellery Channing's biography *Thoreau: The Poet-Naturalist* is published
	Spencer's *The Study of Sociology* is published
1876	Harriet Martineau dies
1883	Karl Marx dies
1884	*Walden* is published in England
1890	Henry Salt publishes *The Life of Henry David Thoreau*, which helps to popularize Thoreau abroad
	The first sociology course is offered by Lester Ward
1892	The first sociology department is founded at the University of Chicago
1894	The first textbook in sociology, *Introduction to the Study of Society*, written by Albion Small and George Vincent, is published
1895	Albion Small founds *American Journal of Sociology*
1906	Gandhi reads Thoreau's works while in prison
1944	Martin Luther King, Jr. reads *Civil Disobedience*

∽

CHAPTER ONE

Disciplinary Disobedience

Reenvisioning Thoreau

A number of groups have placed a claim on Henry David Thoreau. Conservatives argue that he belongs in their camp because he warned against "big government." Liberals believe he fits their mold since he championed the environment and found the materialism of the emerging capitalist society distasteful. Still others are certain that Thoreau's focus on the individual and liberty proves that he would be a Libertarian. Likewise, a variety of academic disciplines have been yoking Thoreauvian thought for a number of years. His American classic *Walden* (1845) is recognized as the quintessential literary description of nature. His explorations of slavery, the role of government, and the duty of citizens in such works as "Civil Disobedience" (1849), "Slavery in Massachusetts" (1854), and "A Plea for Captain John Brown" (1860) are regarded as quintessential examples of independent and critical American political thought. Within the field of economics, Thoreau's works are mined not only for his discourse on work, leisure, slavery, and government, but also for his analysis of the rapid economic changes of his time.[1] More recently, natural historians have focused on lesser-known aspects of Thoreau's intellectual life such as his knowledge and use of science. These historians point out that he had an extensive understanding of botany, engineering, zoology, geology, and meteorology. He was an ardent observer of nature who was not only adept at meticulously recording his observations in journals, but also worked to develop his skills in the methods of scientific inquiry.[2] Beyond academia, and perhaps more well known, Thoreau's writings have been drawn on for global social action and change. In addition to his profound impact on the environmental movement, Thoreau has had a substantial influence on a number of twentieth-century thinkers and social activists, including W. E. B. Du Bois, Mahatma Gandhi, and Dr. Martin Luther King Jr. Thoreau's essay "Civil Disobedience" has inspired the leaders of national political reform and resistance movements in countries such as India, Bulgaria, Holland, England, and the United States.

Thoreau was a poet, philosopher, writer, social critic, surveyor, and, at times, a scientist. He simply defies categorization. In a sense, his "civil disobedience" went beyond the night he spent in jail for not paying his poll tax. As an intellectual he thumbed his nose at all disciplines, as if to say, "Just try to pigeonhole me." But that is exactly what sociology has done with Thoreau and other cross-disciplinary thinkers like him. Most of us would probably not put "sociologist" in the above descriptions of Thoreau, but like many sociologists and social theorists, he most certainly explored immediate issues of everyday life.[3] He addressed a number of sociological concerns—including race, class, industrialization, and social forces—while the field of sociology was in its infancy. *Indeed, prior to the activities of important figures in the history of American sociology, such as Jane Addams, who expounded on the nature of the sociological perspective and methods of social inquiry, Thoreau was engaging in sociological thought and analysis in his own uniquely American way.* And while Thoreau's cultural and academic legacy centers around two topics that are of primary interest to the discipline of sociology—*social change* and *the individual-society relationship*—sociology has not followed in the steps of other disciplines to explore Thoreau's works.

In the following chapters I illustrate five specific ways in which Thoreau's work is relevant and valuable to sociology. I begin in chapter 2 with an examination of *how Thoreau's biographical roots have strong links to important thinkers in the development of sociology and to leaders within the emerging nineteenth-century social science movement in the United States.* In this discussion I review some of the important social changes to which Thoreau was reacting, including the emerging eighteenth-century industrial economy. I also explore the influence important thinkers in the history of sociological thought, such as Jean-Jacques Rousseau, Immanuel Kant, and Adam Smith, had on Thoreau's work. The chapter concludes with a review of Thoreau's important global legacy as a voice for progressive social change. In chapter 3 I move on to address an integral aspect of Thoreauvian social thought: *his strong interest in the ways that major American institutions adversely influenced the individual.* Particular attention is given to Thoreau's analysis of how the industrial capitalist economy structured daily life and individual values, as well as his critique of the American government as a dominant institution that trampled on the individual conscience. Because many who have read Thoreau's work often incorrectly classify it as "Marxian," I have included a brief comparison of Marx and Thoreau, who were contemporaries, but unfamiliar with each other's work.

Chapter 4 follows with an investigation of *Thoreau's analysis of social change, including his deconstruction of American ideals of "progress."* This discussion addresses his inquiry into the socially constructed boundaries between the "civilized" and the "savage," his critique of the ways in which Americans measured "progress," and his evolving views on the need for social reform, as well as the methods to achieve it. Chapter 4 also includes a comparison of Thoreau's approach with those of two theorists whose ideas have been influential on sociological ideas of social development—Herbert Spencer and Emile Durkheim. The focus then shifts in chapter 5 to *the ways in which Thoreau actually went about his social inquiry.* I examine his efforts to "debunk" social life by unveiling the complex meaning behind human behavior, as well as his interest in cultural relativity and social life outside of mainstream American cultural norms and values. I conclude the book in chapter 6 with a discussion of *how Thoreau can help us reimagine the discipline of sociology.* In this final chapter I explore what sociology might learn from other disciplines about understanding and representing social phenomena. I also examine the relationship between the artistic eye and the sociological imagination, as well as the need for sociology to follow Thoreau's lead by approaching social inquiry as a craft, rather than a technical act.

A Sociology of Boundaries

Before moving on to examine Thoreau's ideas in detail, though, it is important to understand why thinkers like him are often neglected by sociology. On the surface, it does seem ironic that a field so occupied with "labeling" and with the "social construction" of concepts such as race and gender has not looked more closely at the pigeonholing of thinkers like Thoreau. However, if we turn a critical eye toward the field of sociology by looking at the social construction of the discipline itself, we will see that the problem of omitting certain thinkers is a logical result of constructing rigid disciplinary categories and boundaries that few people challenge.[4] To understand the exclusionary tendencies of sociology it is necessary to explore the social construction of the discipline, especially the ongoing suspicion of academic sociologists toward "extramural sociologists"—figures outside of formal academic sociology who are nevertheless engaging in sociological work.[5]

Over the last century sociology has institutionalized and constructed a set of standards, criteria, and "ideal types" for what is considered "sociologically" valuable and what is not. In this respect, it is no different from other academic disciplines that have made efforts to become accepted and legitimated. However, it is important to remember that these decisions about who will be examined within sociology and what criteria we should use have been made within a particular historical and social context, and these choices have played a role in constructing a certain type of sociology.[6] The sociology that emerged from this process is, in many ways, less pluralistic and more insulated from many of the other disciplines from which the early sociologists came. In fact, many figures have been excluded from sociological dialogue— artists, writers, and even, until recently, the early female sociologists—even though they engaged in work that is sociological in nature and served important roles as voices for social change.

Exclusionary Theory
In academic sociology, an obvious way to view this isolationist and exclusionary tendency is by tracing the evolution of our theoretical canon and reading lists. Most in-depth texts and readers covering the history and evolution of sociological thought contain a core group of thinkers and schools of thought, as well as the criteria used to justify the inclusion of these particular choices. More often than not, these criteria include figures who have played a major role in the development of formal sociological theory. There are two ironies with such an approach. One is the argument made in a number of theory texts that "only those theorists who have made an impact on the field of sociology are important," which certainly is a perspective that appeals to the same "tradition as authority" approach that the discipline of sociology arose to challenge. The second irony is that many of the earlier theorists were themselves not formally trained in academic sociology. Thorsten Veblen was trained as an economist. Karl Marx studied political economics and law, while Max Weber's background was in history and economics.[7] Herbert Spencer was both a scientist and an engineer before publishing many writings in the *Economist*. Emile Durkheim's background was in philosophy and the bulk of Jane Addams's undergraduate education was in both science and literature. The pluralistic foundation of sociology is a thing of the past.[8] With the exception of a few thinkers, such as Michel Foucault and George Ritzer, the institutionalization of disciplinary boundaries means that in our academic curriculum, and consequently in our classroom discussion, we increasingly like our theorists and others who merit our attention to have been "run through the sociological training machine."

A small number of sociologists have recognized that we risk intellectual stagnation if we function as if only those who fit strictly within the confines of specific criteria have something important to contribute to the discipline. Several theorists have pointed to the exclusion of women social theorists to make a strong case for why the methods of canonization within sociology must be scrutinized. For example, in his book *Classical Sociological Theory* (2000), George Ritzer devotes an entire chapter to female theorists, whom he believes are now only being recognized even though they worked in the same time period as many of their male counterparts who have claimed their own place in the canon. Ritzer even argues that as the result of discrimination, the work of women has been largely ignored. He believes that as their works are rediscovered, their influence will grow over time. Likewise, in their book *Women Founders* (1998) Patricia Lengermann and Jill Niebrugge-Brantley argue not only that the evolution of sociology and its theories has been represented as a history of white male agency, but that this history is a social construction that arose out of the discipline's power arrangements.[9] In their view, the result of selecting some theorists (white males) and delegitimating others (females engaged in applying social science to social activism) created a pattern in sociology that leaned more toward scientism and patriarchal marginalization.

Sociology's Quantitative Fetish

If decreased pluralism can be seen in our theory, it is also present within methods of sociological inquiry, which have become overwhelmingly focused on empirical studies and a more technical approach to understanding social life. The result is that only figures engaging in specialized technical methodologies get recognized as doing important sociological work. Several important sociologists have commented on this increasing tendency of "abstracted empiricism," including C. Wright Mills, who argues in *The Sociological Imagination* (1959) that sociologists often cultivate method for its own sake, which results in the production of facts that are often unrelated to society.[10] In *An Invitation to Sociology* (1963), Peter Berger also writes about the sociologist as a "gatherer of statistics," arguing that many sociological studies were irrelevant to social concern.[11] Both men recognized that an understanding of society was not sociology's birthright and that the discipline did not have a monopoly on the understanding of social phenomena. This fetish of methods, they argue, was obstructive to the possibilities and future of sociology. Mills and Berger called on sociology to align itself closer to the humanities in order to better understand the human condition. Mills believed sociologists should work to develop a playfulness of mind and a release of imagination,[12] while Berger laid out his prescriptions in the form of a craft by encouraging sociologists to study the arts of listening, observing, and writing.[13]

These recommendations for resisting the dominance of empiricism have striking relevance to the work that many "extramural sociologists" have been doing for decades. Indeed, as an external figure Thoreau provides us with a model for what a social inquiry looks like when practiced as "art," or a craft, rather than a technical act. In observing and writing about society, he took a more humanistic approach to exploring social reality that was more in line with the artist than the technical approach of a bureaucratic social researcher. He was able to balance an empirical approach to inquiry with a more "transcendental" way of seeing, by finding a middle ground between the subjective and objective.[14] In fact, he was interested in a science that recognized and joined "subject" and "object."[15] He practiced a number of techniques as a poet and social observer that allowed him to experiment with seeing things from an uncommon view. For example, his prolonged experiment at Walden Pond and the vantage point he adopted and documented as a prisoner in "Civil Disobedience" are just two of his attempts at "seeing the world new."[16] As we will see in the following chapters, Thoreau's example raises some interesting questions for sociology: What can sociology learn from theorists within other fields, such as the arts and the humanities, about observing and representing social reality, and can a place be made for more "literary" thinkers within the field of sociology? What other thinkers had something important to say about society, and who else's ideas are waiting to be discovered?[17] What specific techniques, "ways of seeing," and ways of developing sensory perceptions might sociologists adopt from the artist, journalist, or more literary author? What experiments in observing can be used by sociologists to see common things from uncommon angles?

This type of disciplinary self-reflexivity, questioning, and reformulating of the current rigid construction of our discipline will help us in more complex ways than simply deciding who merits a place in the canon. On a broader level, reforming and relaxing our rigid disciplinary boundaries will help us avoid seeing particular thinkers, like Thoreau, in the binary categories of "sociological" or "not sociological," based on traditional approaches or limited criteria such as the individual's formal academic training. A disciplinary "reformation" like this would help bring broad recognition that important sociological work is not simply raw theory and methods—there are important public sociological works that have for decades received no attention from academic sociology. Lengermann and Niebrugge-Brantley believe that by reaching out to extramural theorists who are "actively engaged with the problems that matter to people in their immediate everyday lives," we can expand "the possibilities for sociology's future."[18] Until such a larger shift occurs, our disciplinary construction will prevent us from examining the very poignant and socially important work that "extramural sociologists" outside of formal sociology are doing. We will also miss out on the important lessons these figures might offer for understanding social phenomena and successfully communicating with the public.

A Path by Which to Tread

It might seem logical that I begin building my case for Thoreau's relevance to sociology by labeling the current criteria, canon, and dialogue on social theorists and others who merit our attention as too rigid and artificial. However, by attacking the current criteria in sociology I am left with a difficult predicament in my effort to make a case for Thoreau. If the current criteria are too rigid, what criteria should be used, and what criteria are appropriate to demonstrate Thoreau's relevance to the field of sociology? Suggesting a set of absolute criteria with which to measure Thoreau from a sociological perspective will do little to expand the overall dialogue within the field. It is necessary to find an overall guiding "spirit" or "consciousness" defining sociology that might be used to analyze Thoreau's relevance to the field. To find such a guide we need look no further than the way in which we teach newcomers about the nature of our discipline.

Beyond Marx, Weber, and Durkheim, the two theorists whose ideas, at their most basic level, are employed to teach the sociological consciousness within undergraduate curriculum are C. Wright Mills and Peter Berger.[19] There are few concepts that are more familiar to sociologists than Mills's "sociological imagination," which is used by most major introductory sociology texts as an introduction to the basic concerns, questions, and approaches of sociology as a discipline.[20] Likewise, Berger's ideas, including the ubiquitous starting point of sociological consciousness—things are not always what they seem—are referenced in most major introductory sociology textbooks. Berger's An Invitation to Sociology and The Social Construction of Reality (1967) have been popular supplementary reading in introductory courses across the United States.[21] I am not suggesting that we use the ideas of these two theorists as a yardstick or as absolute criteria for creating a new canon. However, for the purposes of analyzing Thoreau's work I drew on their ideas as a "lens" to provide a generally accepted context of sociological thought.

Since I am indebted to Mills and Berger for providing a starting point for my analysis of Thoreau's work, it will be helpful to briefly review some of their widely accepted ideas that have provided a foundation on which other sociological concepts are taught within introductory courses and texts. Mills presents his concept of the "sociological imagination" as a form of self-consciousness that suddenly awakens individuals, allowing them to recognize the relationship between biography, fate, and life chances within a particular historical context. He expands on these ideas by discussing the types of questions explored by social analysts and anyone else possessing a sociological imagination. Social analysts typically examine questions of (1) social structure, such as the components of society and their relationships; (2) sociohistorical comparisons, including where a particular society stands in human history; and (3) the prevailing characteristics of the people in a particular society, especially the ways in which their ideas are shaped. These questions occupied a prominent place in the works of the more recognized "classic social analysts" such as Spencer, Durkheim, Marx, and Weber, but were also dominant themes addressed by social theorists whose ideas are only now gaining broader appreciation within the discipline of sociology. These questions and themes are integral not only to sociological inquiry, but also to the manner in which we teach others about the nature of sociological consciousness.

Like those of Mills, Berger's ideas have had a prominent place in undergraduate sociological curriculum, especially in articulating the sociological consciousness as a transformed perspective where individuals find out that "things are not what they seem." Rather than putting forth questions, as Mills does, Berger suggests several characteristics that represent sociological consciousness in action.[22] He argues that a central tenet of sociological thinking is the act of "unmasking" society by looking beyond the "facades of social structures" and questioning commonly accepted goals and social norms.[23] This frame of mind also involves *openness to other ways of thinking*, including an interest in the complexities and components of other cultures and subcultures. It requires that an individual look at society and social reality from *multiple perspectives*, or, as Berger says in his own words, "not only from the perspective of the city hall, but also from that of city jail."[24] Finally, those who possess sociological consciousness recognize the *relativity* of cultural values across time, situation, and location. These ideas correspond directly with fundamental concepts and methods of exploring society that we teach as part of sociological curriculum, such as the deconstruction of traditional norms, skepticism of "common sense," how social location determines values, rejection of ethnocentrism, and how society looks from the vantage point of multiple perspectives. As guiding spirits in my analysis, Mills and

Berger provided a model of questions and themes that many social analysts have asked, as well as the critical thinking methods by which the questions are to be answered.[25] Once again, I used their ideas as a starting point or contextual framework for analysis of Thoreau's work, rather than a stringent set of criteria.

Why Bother with a "Poet-Philosopher"?

There are a number of compelling reasons to wander outside the traditional boundaries of our discipline and follow the lead of other fields that have drawn on Thoreau's work. He was positioned, historically and intellectually, in a way that provides a unique sociological perspective on nineteenth-century American life and beyond. As an interdisciplinary thinker who shares common intellectual and contextual ground with sociology and the social science movement, he provides us with an inside view of American life that differs from well-known accounts by outsiders, such as Harriet Martineau and Alexis de Tocqueville. He developed his own model of society, with a uniquely individualist American approach, by analyzing American social structures and conducting his own sociohistorical comparative analysis. Thoreau is not only one of the most well-known writers of any discipline to address such complex sociological issues as "the individual and society," the social construction of "progress," and social change, he was one of the first American thinkers to write about these subjects. His antimaterialist efforts in *Walden* and his dissenting voice in "Civil Disobedience" certainly represent some of the first uniquely American writing to engage in the "debunking" or "unmasking" tendency that is an inherent trait of the sociological perspective. From the issues he addressed, including class, the environment, government and economics, to the interdisciplinary way in which he went about social inquiry, Thoreau's intellectual range is simply too great for sociology to ignore.

Because sociology has struggled with linking its objectives to a more relevant and effectual "public sociology," there are additional reasons for examining Thoreau. Like other artists and writers, there is no doubt that he succeeded in speaking to the public on important social issues. He is an icon of the environmental, simplicity, and civil rights movements. Thoreau's ability to reach the public conscience certainly originated from his efforts to approach social inquiry as a craft, rather than a technical act, and his ability to communicate these ideas in articulate, meaningful writing. If sociologists hope to become greater agents of change, we can draw on cross-disciplinary figures like Thoreau to reimagine what sociology can be, and we can use him as a means of engaging in healthy disciplinary self-reflection by reconsidering who is allowed to contribute to the dialogue, how we engage in social inquiry, and how we communicate these ideas publicly.

It is likely that this investigation will prove to be challenging or even uncomfortable for readers who are actively engaged in traditional sociology but new to the ideas of Thoreau. Likewise, for those who are already familiar with Thoreau but new to the field of sociology, you are met with the task of viewing Thoreau in a new light and learning about a new discipline. Both journeys come with their own rewards. We can turn to words from Thoreau's essay "Walking" (1862) to find the challenge that lies ahead of us herein:

> What we call knowledge is often our positive ignorance; . . . a man accumulates a myriad of facts, lays them up in his memory, and then in some spring of his life he saunters abroad into great Fields of thought, he as it were goes to grass like a horse, and leaves all his harness behind in the stable. . . . [M]y desire for knowledge is intermittent; but my desire to bathe my head in atmospheres unknown to my feet is perennial and constant.[26]

It is time for Thoreau to saunter into the "field" of sociology, and for sociology to leave its harness behind, put on its own walking shoes and examine its own possibilities by exploring "atmospheres unknown."

Notes

1. See Christopher Bodily, "Henry David Thoreau: The Instrumental Transcendentalist?" *Journal of Economic Issues* 21, no. 1 (1987): 203–18; John Diggins, "Thoreau, Marx and the Riddle of Alienation," *Social Research* 39, no. 4 (1972): 571–98; Leonard Neufeldt, *The Economist: Henry Thoreau and Enterprise* (New York: Oxford University Press, 1989).

2. See Laura Dassaw Walls, *Seeing New Worlds: Henry David Thoreau and Nineteenth-Century Natural Science* (Madison: University of Wisconsin Press, 1995).

3. These are the words of Patricia Lengermann and Jill Niebrugge-Brantley, who argue in *The Women Founders: Sociological and Social Theory 1830–1930* (Boston: McGraw-Hill, 1998) that the basic task of sociology is to speak to the most immediate problems confronting society.

4. Lengermann and Niebrugge-Brantley, *Women Founders*, 2.

5. Charles Lemert, *Sociology after the Crisis* (Boulder, CO: Westview, 1995), 207.

6. To read others making the same argument see Geoffrey Hawthorn's "No Context, No History: The Sociological Canon," in *Canon vs. Culture: Reflections on the Current Debate*, ed. Jan Gorak, 43–45 (New York: Garland, 2001); and Lengermann and Niebrugge-Brantley, *Women Founders*, 1998.

7. Steven Rosenthal, "An Egalitarian Course in Classical Sociological Theory," The Etext Archives, 1995, www.etext.org/Politics/Progressive.Sociologists/

marthas-corner/Rosenthal:Egalitarian_Course_in_Classical_Sociology (accessed July 10, 2002).

8. Christopher Wilkes, "A Modest Proposal Indeed," *Perspectives: Newsletter of the ASA Theory Section* 28, no. 3 (February 2006): 7–9.

9. Lengermann and Brantley, *Women Founders*, 2.

10. C. Wright Mills, *The Sociological Imagination* (New York: Oxford University Press, 1959), 24.

11. Peter Berger, *An Invitation to Sociology: A Humanistic Perspective* (New York: Bantam/Doubleday, 1963), 8.

12. Mills, *The Sociological Imagination*, 215.

13. See Berger, *Invitation to Sociology*, 1963.

14. H. Daniel Peck, *Thoreau's Morning Work: Memory and Perception in "A Week on the Concord and Merrimack Rivers," "The Journal," and "Walden"* (New Haven, CT: Yale University Press, 1990).

15. Laura Dassow Walls, "Introduction: The Man Most Alive," in *Material Faith: Henry David Thoreau on Science*, ed. Laura Walls and J. Parker Huber (Boston: Mariner Original, 1999), xi.

16. Henry David Thoreau, "Huckleberries," in *The Natural History Essays*, ed. Robert Sattelmayer (Salt Lake City, UT: Peregrine Smith, 1980), 254.

17. This question, raised by Patricia Lengermann and Jill Niebrugge-Brantley in the first chapter of *Women Founders*, is the fundamental starting point of this book and should remain a perpetual concern for all sociologists.

18. Lengermann and Brantley, *Women Founders*, 310.

19. While seeking out a "guiding spirit" for this project, I came across David Kessel's unpublished work on the use of Peter Berger and C. Wright Mills to explore the ideas of Erich Fromm from a sociological perspective. Kessel, "Fromm, Mills, Berger and Sociology," The Sociology Shop, 2002, www.angelfire.com/or/sociologyshop/fromills.html (accessed May 10, 2002).

20. Kessel, "Fromm, Mills, Berger and Sociology."

21. Kessel, "Fromm, Mills, Berger and Sociology."

22. In *An Invitation to Sociology* Berger calls these characteristics the debunking, relativization, unrespectability, and cosmopolitan motifs.

23. Berger, *An Invitation to Sociology*, 38.

24. Berger, *An Invitation to Sociology*, 47.

25. Kessel, "Fromm, Mills, Berger and Sociology."

26. Henry David Thoreau, "Walking," in *The Portable Thoreau*, rev. ed., ed. Carl Bode (New York: Penguin, 1987), 623.

CHAPTER TWO

~

The Seeds and Fruit of
Thoreauvian Thought

Thoreau was born in Concord, Massachusetts, in 1817.[1] Originally named David Henry, the "staunch individualist" later reversed his first and middle names in the mid-1830s. This was perhaps an early indication of his lifelong fascination with wordplay, as well as a move to demonstrate his individuality.[2] His father became a successful pencil manufacturer, and his mother, along with other family members, was active in the antislavery movement. Of the four Thoreau children, Henry was chosen to attend college, entering Harvard in 1833. While there he read widely in classic and modern languages as well as intellectual and natural philosophy. By the time he finished Harvard, Thoreau was reading in Greek, Latin, Italian, French, and German. Following his graduation in 1837, he briefly taught school, but was fired because he disliked the use of corporal punishment. That same year he began a close friendship with Ralph Waldo Emerson, who introduced Thoreau to his intellectual circle. German writers such as Kant, Hegel, and Goethe were essential reading within this group, which included Transcendentalists Bronson Alcott and Theodore Parker. For better and worse, Emerson served as Thoreau's mentor, particularly in advising Thoreau on his writing career and intellectual endeavors.

From 1838 to 1844 Thoreau "sauntered" through life, trying out a number of different jobs and residences. He attempted to open a school, worked for his father's pencil-making business, and made several excursions to Maine with his brother, John. During this time Thoreau also began lecturing before the Concord Lyceum and writing for the *Dial*, a Transcendentalist publication edited by Emerson and Margaret Fuller. Between taking up residence at the Emersons' (1841–1843) and moving back in with his own family (1844–1845), Thoreau moved to Staten Island to tutor Emerson's nephew and to make publishing connections in New York. It was on Independence Day of 1845 that Thoreau moved into the cabin on Walden Pond where he would live for two years in an effort to "front the essential facts of life."[3] In addition to observing nature and pondering the necessities of life, it was during this time that Thoreau spent a night in jail for refusing to pay a poll tax, an action that later inspired him to write "Civil Disobedience." While at the pond Thoreau journaled regularly and also completed drafts of A Week on the Concord and Merrimack Rivers and Walden.

After departing the cabin in 1847 he moved back in with the Emersons and succeeded over the next few years in publishing several works. "Resistance to Civil Government" appeared in Aesthetic Papers (1849) and A Week on the Concord and Merrimack Rivers (1849) was published by James Munroe of Boston. A Week did poorly, and Thoreau later wrote in his journal, "I now have a library of nearly 900 volumes over 700 of which I wrote myself."[4] In the early 1850s Thoreau became active in the abolitionist movement, eventually presenting a lecture in 1854 entitled "Slavery in Massachusetts" at an abolitionist meeting in Framingham, Massachusetts. That same year, the prestigious publishing house Ticknor & Fields published Walden, which met with moderate success, eventually selling out its first printing in 1859. Thoreau continued to work as a surveyor, lecturer, and writer in the latter half of the 1850s. He also remained active in the antislavery movement, meeting the radical abolitionist John Brown in 1857. Two years later Thoreau publicly spoke in defense of Brown, who was condemned to hang for leading a raid on a federal arsenal in Harpers Ferry, West Virginia. In 1860, while engaging in a nature experiment, Thoreau caught a cold that eventually led to bronchitis, and then tuberculosis. He died in 1862, at the age of forty-four. By that time he had amassed enough writing to fill thousands of pages of journals, and had published works in a number of publications, including Putnam's Monthly, the Democratic Review, and the Atlantic Monthly.

Thoreau's Social and Intellectual Context: Common Soil with Sociology

Thoreau was a uniquely American figure who is well known around the world as a literary master, champion of nature, and staunch individualist. His most well-known acts—retreating to Walden Pond and refusing to pay a poll tax, which resulted in jail time—are the ultimate examples of a conscious and independent thinking individual. Yet, as much as Thoreau's individuality stands out, it is important to examine the environment of his biography. To use a Thoreauvian metaphor, we need to explore the "seeds" and "roots" of his work. In doing so we find that his ideas, writings and actions were shaped within a context of sweeping social change and new intellectual currents. On both fronts Thoreau actually shares common soil with some of the roots of sociology. In fact, the social changes that influenced Thoreau's environment and work—such as a burgeoning industrial society, as well as political and social reform—are the same that shaped the ideas of important thinkers in the development of sociological theory during the nineteenth and early twentieth centuries, including Karl Marx, Emile Durkheim, Max Weber, and Jane Addams. Likewise, if we explore how Thoreau's immediate intellectual environment shaped his life's work, we find that his intellectual lineage can also be linked to some of the roots of sociology. A number of figures in his immediate social circle became involved in the Associationist Social Science movement of the nineteenth century. More importantly, though, he was exposed to a number of intellectual movements and ideas, including German and Eastern thought, Transcendentalism, Romanticism, and the emerging fields of science, such as botany, ornithology, and zoology. Through several of these influences, especially Transcendentalism and Romanticism, Thoreau's intellectual lineage can be traced back to important thinkers in the development of sociological theory, such as Kant and Rousseau. This context of rapid social and intellectual changes in which he found himself helped to lay the groundwork for his expansive intellectual canvas and far-reaching interests, which included society, the individual, and nature.

Social Forces

It has been said that Thoreau "only felt himself in opposition";[5] there is no doubt that during his lifetime there was much for the "crank-poet" to resist and challenge. The forces of modernity served as his muse—both America and Europe were experiencing rapid social change, as technology, reform, and conflict reshaped everyday life. American society in particular was experiencing growth and transition throughout all of its major social institutions. Industrialization was altering the workplace, railroads and mills were changing the landscape, and capitalist ethos was transforming social values toward fashion and money. In Thoreau's New England, urbanization and manufacturing were on the rise. The creation of large economic bureaucracies, along with advances such as the railroad, the steam engine, and the telegraph, provided efficient means of getting products to the consumer. Coupled with the agricultural crisis in Europe, the job opportunities available in the

United State brought rapid demographic changes to the young nation. Between Irish and German immigration and the annexation of Mexico, the population doubled during Thoreau's lifetime. The treaty to end the war with Mexico had allowed the annexation of Texas, New Mexico, Arizona, and California, which heightened the debate over slavery and states' rights. The doctrine of "manifest destiny" and the gold rush of the late 1840s cemented westward expansion into the national consciousness. America's government was evolving in the wake of physical changes to the nation's population and borders. The modern Democratic and Republican parties were but infants, and were contenders with the reform-oriented Whigs and the xenophobic Know-Nothing Party. Aside from the American government, another authority was emerging in the nineteenth century as a prominent method of knowledge: science. Advances in a number of scientific fields, including medicine, as well as the publication works such as Darwin's *Origin of Species* (1859), strengthened the institutionalization of science in American culture.

The changes Thoreau witnessed did not just include social structures, such as the American political system or the economy: the character of the American public was also being transformed and challenged, especially social norms and values. The new mass production that was made possible by industrialization required mass consumption, which meant that the creation of modern consumer values was a necessity. Newer ideals of fashion, progress, and wealth were emerging among the American public during the nineteenth century, especially a desire to accumulate consumer goods. In addition to these new economic values, other cultural shifts had already begun by the 1820s. Reform efforts were taking root in the social fabric of America as abolition, women's rights, and labor movements were challenging dominant values about race, gender, and work life. Abolitionist organizations were founded in Boston and Philadelphia in the early 1830s, and a few decades later Harriet Beecher Stowe's *Uncle Tom's Cabin* (1852) successfully portrayed the human side of slavery to the American public. Campaigns for women's rights were also becoming more prominent and influential. Thoreau's fellow Transcendentalist Margaret Fuller raised critical questions about the institution of marriage and sexual division of labor in her popular book *Woman in the Nineteenth Century* (1845). Other important publications, such as the *Revolution*, gave leaders of the women's movement, such as Elizabeth Cady Stanton and Lucy Stone, a public venue to advocate for women's education and voting rights. With Stanton's help, national women's conventions began in 1848, broadening publicity and participation in the movement.

These social changes were the context in which Thoreau was writing and to which he was reacting. The influence of these transitions can be seen in most of Thoreau's writings, including the more celebrated works of *Walden* and "Civil Disobedience," where he explored the emerging values of a consumer society, definitions of progress, the issue of slavery, reform, and the relationship between the citizen and government.

Intellectual Context

Although Thoreau responded, as an intellectual and a citizen, to these broader changes around him, intellectual currents he came in contact with through his immediate environment and intellectual circle also influenced his work and agenda. If we examine these influences and his intellectual lineage, we can again see how the seeds of Thoreauvian thought are actually rooted in the some of the same "soil" from which sociology arose. Several of the movements and thinkers that played an integral part in shaping the early stages of sociology and sociological theory also shaped and influenced Thoreau's work. He was profoundly influenced by the Romantic and Transcendental movements, which had their roots in Rousseau, Kant, and David Hume. Thoreau also reacted to the works of Adam Smith—much of his protest to Smith's *Wealth of Nations* (1776) can be found in the first and longest chapter of *Walden*.[6] Mainstay Thoreauvian concerns—such as the state of nature, the relationship of the individual to society, and the necessities of life—are a direct result of these influences. However, even though Thoreau held steadfast to many of the tenets of the Romantic movement, he was also intrigued by—and experimented with—the scientific methods the Enlightenment had brought forth. He was impressed with the works of Charles Darwin, had an appreciation for measurement and mechanics, and became a skilled observer of natural and social phenomena, taking copious notes on what he saw.[7] An examination of how these movements and thinkers influenced Thoreau's intellectual activity will not only provide insight into the seeds of Thoreau's social thought, it will also allow us to understand how Thoreau relates to sociology and to contextualize his ideas within the historical development of the field.

Enlightenment, Romanticism, and Transcendentalism

Before Thoreau was born, the Enlightenment (1689–1789) had already become heavily influential around the world, particularly in Britain, Germany, France, and the United States. The movement ushered in critical examination of social order and institutions that restricted human capability, such as political systems and the church.[8] Enlightenment thinkers also extended this sense of scrutiny to the individual by valuing self-examination as a means of personal development. The social reformers who spearheaded this movement put their faith not in tradition or religion, but in science and reason as means for humans to gain personal and social freedom. Believing there was an order to the universe, they aimed to understand it so that progressive change could be made. This was done by combining rational thought with observation in the form of the scientific method, and by using the senses to collect data. Enlightenment thinkers such as Sir Isaac Newton pioneered advances in mathematics, physics, and astronomy and proved that a methodological and practical understanding of the universe was possible.[9]

These ideas played a substantial role in the subsequent development of sociology, but how do they relate to Thoreau? The Enlightenment became the foundation of many of the intellectual movements of the nineteenth century, laying the groundwork for further critical social thought.[10] It had particular influence on the Romantic movement, which directly shaped Thoreau's work. Yet many are unaware that Thoreau was also very intrigued by the new scientific understanding that resulted from the Enlightenment. His advanced knowledge of scientific methods and the ways in which he used them to explore the world around him will be examined in later in this chapter, as well as chapters 4 and 5.

Transcendentalism is the intellectual movement with which Thoreau is most often associated. An understanding of this movement is of particular importance for several reasons. First, it was the immediate intellectual circle in which Thoreau traveled: He wrote, lived, studied, and lectured among other Transcendentalists, including poet and playwright Emily Dickinson as well as Emerson and Fuller, who were introduced to each other by the sociologist Harriet Martineau. Many of the basic ideas and values of the Transcendentalism had a strong impact on Thoreau's social critique, including the institutions he chose to scrutinize. Second, it is through Transcendentalism that we can trace Thoreau's intellectual lineage and find strong connections to early thinkers in the development of sociology. The ideas of Kant, Rousseau, and Romanticism were brought to Thoreau through his involvement in the popular intellectual and reform movement. Prominent in New England from 1836 to 1860, Transcendentalism initially emerged as a response to the secularization of a society fascinated with science and technology, and as a reaction to the conservative shifts taken by American Unitarian and Calvinist churches.[11] Transcendentalists believed strongly in the reliability of the human conscience, and held an absolute faith in the individual above all else. Their strong celebration of the individual came from the idea that within each person lay clues about nature, the universe, and God.[12] This led Transcendentalists to accept that all knowledge about the universe begins with knowledge of the self. They believed that through education, contemplation, reflection, and observation, a greater consciousness of reality could be attained. Most Transcendentalists focused on the natural world as a source of symbolic meaning, illumination, and spiritual instruction.[13] Nature was seen as an outward representation of the human mind and was a place of spiritual reflection, education, and meaning.

Because Transcendentalists believed that self-realization and reform began with self-examination, they advocated for an appropriate relationship between the individual and society. Roles imposed on the individual by society and its institutions impeded individual expression and freedom, restricted choice, and ultimately resulted in self-alienation.[14] Transcendentalists believed that if we understood the roles and demands that society imposed on the individual, we could move from a false understanding of ourselves to a more authentic existence. Each person, Transcendentalists argued, should be free to pursue self-development over the demands that society places on every individual.[15] However, while the New England Transcendentalists stressed individual freedom and autonomy, they did not encourage social isolation. Much of their work brought their members into society, rather than out of it.[16] As a result, a number of followers within the movement focused on the great issues of the time.[17] Transcendentalists expressed their philosophy through lecturing and a broad range of social reform activities.[18] Since they were more politically active than many of the other writers of their time, their ideas threatened a number of social institutions, including the church.[19] Though the movement began in New England, it eventually spread throughout American culture by way of the literature and essays produced by its members, as well as their involvement in reform activities that included women's rights, adult education, kindergarten, and abolition.

Transcendentalism, in turn, was heavily influenced by Romanticism. As a movement, Romanticism emerged in reaction to the Enlightenment's focus on rationality and order, instead espousing subjectivity, passion, imagination, individualism, emotion over reason, and sense over intellect.[20] To the Romantics, faith and intuition were essential to understanding society. The movement brought a strong shift from objective to more subjective ways of knowing. Many of the thinkers within the movement saw nature as a way to learn about "natural man" and the primitive. They were also quick to advocate for liberty as well as intellectual and spiritual revolution.[21] The Romantics' intense celebration of the individual led to a preoccupation with the arts, such as poetry, painting, and music, as a way to communicate the personal experience of the "common man" in a representative manner.[22] Some of the groundwork for the Romantic movement was laid by two Enlightenment thinkers with whom Thoreau was familiar—Rousseau and Kant. Kant believed that the mind was, by nature, a creative and active entity that played a role in sensory experience; therefore, he argued, the mind must be freed from its dependence on external sources for knowledge.[23] While other thinkers of the Enlightenment held to a more deterministic approach, Kant believed this did not allow for human creativity.[24] His move from objective ways of knowing to more subjective methods was a reaction to the ideas of thinkers such as John Locke, who believed that the human mind was passive. Instead, Kant believed in a "Transcendental logic"—knowledge was found in the subjectiveness of human thinking, rather than in the objects of experience. In fact, Kant coined the term "transcendentalism" in his groundbreaking metaphysical work *Critique of Pure Reason* (1781).[25]

Another precursor to the Romantic movement, and an individual whose ideas parallel Thoreau's closely, was Rousseau. He was primarily concerned with the idea of "natural man" and the methods used to deduce his characteristics, but he also explored the origins and consequences of society and modernity, and the possibilities of social change.[26] To Rousseau, like the Romantics, freedom was fundamental and the perfection of the individual was possible. First, though, individuals needed to understand the laws of nature in order to fit the most appropriate social order to natural law. Since Rousseau believed that humans in nature were devoid of social and cultural traits, he wanted to devise a method to determine the characteristics of "natural man" that would guide the process of social change.[27] These methods included studying primitive people and observing animals in their natural habitat.[28] In contrast to thinkers such as Thomas Hobbes and John Locke, Rousseau believed that it was civil society, not nature, that gave rise to problems and war. Since human needs were simple, he argued, the individual did not need a large amount of resources or property. Rousseau was an Enlightenment thinker, but his move away from the Enlightenment's heavy reliance on rationality toward a strong faith in the individual conscience helped lay the groundwork for the newer ideas of Romanticism.[29]

Cultivating a Model of Society

These social and intellectual contexts of rapid social change and a rich and varied intellectual circle certainly planted the seeds for Thoreau's ideas and activities, but how did Thoreau bear fruit from these ideas, and which ones did he incorporate into his own work? How do these movements and thinkers relate to his mission as an intellectual and a writer? Understanding Thoreau's social thought—his model of society—begins with answering these questions. Compared to European contemporaries who analyzed social life, such as Karl Marx, Thoreau's analysis was uniquely American in its emphasis on the individual. Indeed, building on the influences of Rousseau, Kant, Transcendentalism, and Romanticism, Thoreau's unit of analysis was the individual, not society. Because the individual was most sacred, Thoreau's social analysis began with explorations of the ways in which the individual related to and was influenced by society. He believed that society—depending on the way it was structured—could severely restrain and corrupt the individual. The true individual freedom that he sought for himself and argued for in his writings required self-exploration, a process that he and other Transcendentalists saw as imperative to a well-lived life. Through exploring our own lives, he believed, we could understand how society often creates barriers to self-development and cultivation; this type of self-exploration could bring individual reform and freedom from the restraints of society. We can see this type of analysis as a prominent theme in much of Thoreau's writing. *Walden*, "Civil Disobedience," and "Slavery in Massachusetts" are all well known for their examination of the relationship between individual and society and for Thoreau's emphasis on using self-examination as a method of transcending some of the negative effects of society.

Nature and "Natural Man"

In addition to the individual, Thoreau also held nature as sacred. Like other Transcendentalists and Romantics, he looked to nature as an arena of education on the universe and the self. Nature could function as a tool of reflection to reveal "higher truths."[30] To Thoreau, nature's utility was not simply abstract or spiritual: It had a "sensate," material significance.[31] Some of his views on nature, as well as his interest in the effects of society on the individual, can be traced back through Transcendentalism and Romanticism to the ideas of Rousseau. Like Rousseau, Thoreau was interested in "natural man" and in ways to determine the characteristics of humans who are not affected by the influences of society.[32] Both men believed that in the state of nature humans were innately good; it was society that altered the character of the individual. Thoreau, like Rousseau, believed that humans could revisit innate characteristics that had been destroyed by social institutions by seeking harmony with nature and wilderness:

> I love nature partly *because* she is not man, but a retreat from him. None of his institutions control or pervade her. There is a different kind of right that prevails. In her midst I can be glad with an entire gladness. If this world were all a man, I could not stretch myself, I should lose all hope. He is constraint, she is freedom to me. He makes me wish for another world. She makes me content

with this. None of the joys she supplies is subject to his rules and definitions. What he touches he taints. In thought he moralizes.[33]

Rousseau and Thoreau believed that an understanding of the laws of nature would help inform individual self-realization as well as social change. They even shared methods of exploring the pre-social individual. Rousseau studied more primitive people and the behavior of animals as a method of insight into natural man. Thoreau studied the American Indian and even recorded and analyzed the behavior of animals for *Walden*. Perhaps more than any other figure, Thoreau believed strongly that nature, an arena he saw as the antithesis of modern society, was just as functionally important to society as many of the so-called essential social institutions of the day.

Thoreau's interest in the relationship between human and nature and his beliefs about the important social functions of nature had a strong influence on his analysis of society. He was motivated to explore aspects of social life that corrupted proper human relations with nature, including the physical destruction of nature for profit and the ways in which humans became pre-occupied with other, less important concerns. Most of his well-known writings echo these themes. *Walden* does not just include his deep celebration of nature, it also contains his intense scrutiny of capitalism's transformation of nature into a lifeless commodity to be bought and sold in the marketplace. *The Maine Woods* (1864) chronicles Thoreau's travels far into the bowels of nature, including his own search for true wilderness, his appreciation for American Indians, and the important lessons that could be learned in the wilderness. Building on the ideas of thinkers such as Rousseau, Thoreau used nature not only as a window into the pre-social human, but also as an arena and tool to ponder and critique the consequences of modern social life.

Social Institutions

While Thoreau held firmly to the Transcendental and Romantic notions of individuality, he did not wish to throw out the concept of society altogether.[34] The individual was his primary unit of social analysis, but he did have a strong interest in social institutions. Unlike figures such as Durkheim and Spencer, though, Thoreau was not interested in the ways that social institutions function for the good of society as a whole; rather, his analysis was centered on how social institutions did or, more often, did not function for the good of the individual. His analysis of social institutions, then, was also firmly wedded to his ideals of progress. Since Thoreau's model of society equated progress with the sovereignty of the individual conscience, any efforts by social institutions to "regulate" individual morality, norms, or behavior was seen as regressive social development.

Indeed, the main conflict of society, he observed, was that its institutions unjustly tried to exact their influences on the individual conscience. His frustration with an American society that swallowed the individual is evident in *Walden*:

> Nevertheless, this points to an important distinction between the civilized man and the savage; and, no doubt, they have designs on us for our benefit, in making the life of a civilized people an *institution*, in which the life of an individual is to a great extent absorbed, in order to preserve and perfect that of the race. But I wish to show at what a sacrifice this advantage is at present obtained, and to suggest that we may possibly so live as to secure all the advantage without suffering any of the disadvantage.[35]

Given his dissatisfaction with the characteristics of American society, he set out to remove the false consciousness of individuals, so they could see how social institutions often restrict self-development. He critiqued the institutions that most suppressed the individual—government, the American economy, slavery, education, and religion—by revealing the illusions that allowed them to function as well as the emptiness behind their promises to the citizen and consumer.[36] Thoreau wanted to improve and reorder society by awakening the reader to life as an individual, and to secure the advantages of society and modernity while doing away with the disadvantages.

While many around the world saw American democracy as an experimental form of government that symbolized the ultimate freedom, Thoreau believed this view was a myth. He recognized that the American government held the most forceful power as a social institution, particularly in its ability to influence the individual on a corporeal level. Indeed, along with the economy, the American government played a significant role in what Thoreau saw as the ultimate sin against the individual: slavery. Yet the government also demanded the allegiance of the conscience. In the so-called Land of Liberty the citizen was required to acquiesce his or her individual will to that of the government with the understanding that government would act in the interest of all. To Thoreau, this flawed relationship was a prime example of the problematic utilitarian structure of most social institutions.

If the government as social institution represented an affront to the individual conscience, another social institution was an equal transgressor: the American economy. Because of the rapid and far-reaching economic changes during his lifetime, Thoreau was concerned with the ways in which the ideas of economists and industrial capitalism were altering daily life.[37] His critique of the American economy as a principal social institution can be traced back to the ideals he held as a result of his Transcendental and Romantic influences—the subjective experience, individual liberty, self-actualization, and self-reliance. From this perspective, industrial capitalism was one of the most egregious offenders of the individual conscience. Just as he did with the American government, Thoreau turned commercial lifestyle on its head, portraying it as a hindrance and an illusion, rather than a social improvement. As a social institution, the economy instilled anxiety in individuals by encouraging them to organize their lives around commodities. The marketplace, especially through division of labor, dehumanized and objectified individuals, relegating them to simple cogs or parts in a larger "machine" of production.

However, Thoreau's analysis of the economy as a social institution was not just influenced by his Romantic and Transcendental roots. He was quite familiar with the works of Adam Smith, whose *Wealth of Nations* was published in 1776. Robert D. Richardson Jr., who has written an exhaustive intellectual biography of Thoreau, points out that Thoreau disagreed with Smith on a number of issues, and that Thoreau's first chapter of *Walden*, "Economy," is actually a reaction to Smith's ideas on the economy.[38] While Smith championed capitalism, division of labor, and increased consumption, Thoreau believed that all of these dehumanized and alienated the individual.[39] Instead Thoreau idealized self-sufficiency, which was accomplished by living simply and not buying into the traps of luxury items or other goods that required extensive exchange, lengthy work time, or division of labor.[40] Thoreau's time at Walden was, in part, a protest to demonstrate the virtues of self-reliance as a path to self-cultivation. It was self-reliance, not dependence on others for exchange and services, that would allow for the simplistic lifestyle necessary to engage in self-exploration.[41]

Thoreau as Scientist?

Despite his Transcendental and Romantic roots, Thoreau was also influenced by the Enlightenment. Though he heavily critiqued some of the effects of modernity, he certainly was not a luddite, nor a sworn enemy of technology and science. In fact, a lesser-known realm of Thoreau's intellectual life is his understanding and use of scientific methods. He was a land surveyor, pencil maker, and keen observer of natural phenomena. Although Transcendentalism was opposed to science, Thoreau was fascinated by technology and often used science to illuminate his ideas and writings.[42] Some even argue that Thoreau was a Transcendentalist and scientist simultaneously.[43] He uniquely synthesized the ideas of the Enlightenment together with Transcendentalism and Romanticism with one mission in mind—to awaken the reader to world that surrounds us, natural and social: "The question is not what you look at, but how you look and whether you see."[44]

Thoreau became so interested in the abilities of science to express thought and provide "sight," or to give voice to all phenomena, that he actively attempted to integrate several disciplines into a synthesized approach.[45] Laura Walls, who has illuminated the more scientific side of Thoreau's work, believes that interdisciplinary integration was Thoreau's attempt to "give voice to all agents that created the world he knew, human and non-human, present, future and past," and to "reach a connective truth through the commonplace particulars of daily life in a place exemplary only in its ordinaries."[46] Thoreau's ideas on this mission are clear through his writings:

> Every man tracks himself through life, in all his hearing and reading and observation and traveling. His observations make a chain. The phenomena or fact that cannot in any wise be linked with the rest which he has observed, he does not observe.[47]

Walls points out that Thoreau engaged in a number of different scientific activities.[48] Under the label of natural philosophy he studied mechanics, astronomy, optics, and electricity. He also measured and recorded countless natural phenomena and collected and labeled species, some of which he sent to Louis Agassiz, a well-known zoologist who worked at Harvard in the late 1840s. Thoreau did become disenchanted with the increased objectivity of science, since it often eliminated the personality and capacities of the investigator from investigation.[49] However, he engaged in a number of activities using the systematic methods he had learned from science, including a detailed study of American Indian culture and history. By the time of his death he had taken thousands of notes on American Indians, including accounts from visitors, travelers, explorers, and missionaries, in an effort to compile one of the first scientific accounts of an Indian tribe.[50] He spent time taking field notes on their cooking methods, canoes, and trap construction. His other observations of American social life informed his writings on slavery, government, and capitalism.

Thoreau was certainly far more familiar with empiricism and pure scientific methodology than many of the social critics and social theorists of his time. However, his fascination with both science and society did not lead to a full-blown social scientific approach, in the modern sense. Given the time period in which he lived, though, this should come as no surprise. During Thoreau's lifetime, social science in general was far from the organized and systematic endeavor that it would become in the twentieth century. Nevertheless, Thoreau was not only on the cusp of combining his interests in science and society, he actually had immediate connections through his intellectual circles to many figures who were heavily involved in the emerging social science movement of nineteenth-century America.

Thoreau in the Historical Context of the Emergence of Sociology in the United States

To place Thoreau in the historical context of the emergence of sociology in the United States, we need look no further than his immediate social and intellectual circle. Indeed, he was in the midst of the emerging social science scene in the nineteenth century. The Transcendentalist movement had links to Associationist social science, which laid the foundation for a social science movement in the United States by initiating the transition in social thought from theological to scientific thinking.[51] Associationist social science emerged in the 1840s and eventually held conventions, published a journal, and established utopian communities known as phalanxes. The Associationists had adopted the ideas of Charles Fourier, a French businessman, who believed in association communities where all labor was equally compensated and organized around the talents of individual community members.[52] Members of the Associationist movement put forth their own theory of society, history, and human nature. Like Thoreau, they critiqued the emerging social structure of nineteenth-century America, especially industrial capitalism.

Though not a member of the Associationist movement, Thoreau was situated in its "currents."[53] He visited and was invited to join Brook Farm, a Transcendentalist utopian commune that later became the headquarters of the Associationists. A number of articles about Brook Farm appeared in the *Dial*, the Transcendentalist journal that published more than forty of Thoreau's pieces and that he helped Emerson to edit. In 1843 while he was working as a tutor to Emerson's nephew in New York, Thoreau met several leaders of the Associationist movement, including Albert Brisbane, W. H. Channing, and Horace Greeley. Brisbane wrote *Association* (1843) and *The Social Destiny of Man* (1840), which Emerson reviewed in the *Dial*. Brisbane also founded the *Phalanx, or the Journal of Social Science*, and went on to publish *Sociological Series* in 1876. Horace Greeley founded the *New York Tribune*, in which he promoted Brisbane and the ideas of Associationist social science. Greeley became a lifelong supporter of Thoreau and worked to place several of his essays in reputable publications. In New York, Thoreau also met W. H. Channing, who was a leader within the Associationist movement and a student of Comte's ideas and positivism. It was Channing who helped to turn Transcendentalist members of Brook Farm on to Associationist ideology.

Members of Thoreau and Emerson's immediate circle in Concord were also involved with Associationist social science, including F. B. Sanborn, George Ripley, and Theodore Parker. Of these three, Thoreau was closest to Sanborn, whom he met and befriended in 1855. When Sanborn began boarding with the Thoreaus, the two saw each other on a daily basis for several years and often walked together around Concord. Sanborn was one of the first to discuss Darwin with Thoreau, soon after the publication of *Origin of Species*.[54] Sanborn also encouraged Thoreau's interest in John Brown, the passionate abolitionist who led a militant raid at Harpers Ferry, West Virginia, in 1859. As part of the "secret six," Sanborn knew about Brown's plan for the Harpers Ferry raid before it occurred. Although Thoreau was unaware of plans for the raid, he later helped Sanborn smuggle one of John Brown's men to Canada.[55] Sanborn went on to help found the American Social Science Association and served as editor of its journal from 1867 to 1897. In the 1890s he played an important role in popularizing Thoreau by editing a number of Thoreau's unpublished works and writing several important pieces about him, including a biography.[56]

As the Associationist movement was gaining momentum, the ideas of Auguste Comte and positivism were moving from Europe to the United States. Harriet Martineau's translation of Comte's work appeared in 1853, but the first reference to Comte in the United States occurred in the *New Jerusalem* magazine in 1840.[57] The second reference to Comte, written by the Transcendentalist and Associationist Theodore Parker, actually appeared in the *Dial* in 1842, a year before Thoreau began helping Emerson to edit the Transcendentalist magazine. Parker, Ripley, and O. A. Brownson, all members of Thoreau and Emerson's circle, eagerly discussed Comte's work with others, including W. H. Channing.[58] Though he did not write about Comte, it is likely that Thoreau would have been familiar with references to his work, including an anonymous writer's discussion of Comte that was published in *Putnam's Monthly* (1854), a magazine founded by fellow Transcendentalist George Putnam, in which Thoreau published *An Excursion to Canada* and parts of *Walden* in 1853, as well as *Cape Cod* in 1855. Comte's influence on social thought in America increased greatly with Martineau's translation of his works (1853) and reached its peak in the late 1850s.[59]

The 1860s brought a decline in Comte's influence on American social thought, as the ideas of Spencer and Darwin were beginning to gain recognition.[60] Several individuals in Thoreau's circle were more than familiar with Spencer's work. Emerson met with Spencer in 1842 and, along with Spencer, Walt Whitman, Mark Twain, Andrew Carnegie, and others, founded the Twilight Club. Fellow Transcendentalist O. A. Brownson later wrote an in-depth article about Spencer for *Catholic World* (1866). The Transcendentalists also knew Harriet Martineau, as a friend, fellow reformer, and intellectual. Like the Transcendentalists, Martineau was active in the American abolition movement, and was accepted into the Transcendentalist community during her visit to America from 1834 to 1836. It was Martineau who introduced Emerson and Margaret Fuller, an important female in the Transcendentalist movement who also collaborated with Emerson to edit the *Dial*. Other contemporaries who were writing at the same time as Thoreau and who would prove to be important in sociological thought are Alexis de Tocqueville and Karl Marx. Tocqueville's *Democracy in America* was published in two parts (1835 and 1840) and was received warmly in the United States shortly after it was published. Unlike Thoreau, Tocqueville decried individualism in the United States as a liability. Marx published a number of important works between 1840 and 1860. Though Marx and Thoreau were writing at the same time and share similarities in their critiques of capitalism, neither was familiar with the works of the other. Marx's writings were largely overlooked in the United States, and did not become influential in American sociology until after the mid-twentieth century.[61]

Thoreau died in 1862, before the growth of a legitimate and formal academic sociological scene. Nearly thirty years would pass before Lester Ward would offer the first sociology course (1890), the University of Chicago would start a sociology department (1892), and Albion W. Small would found the *American Journal of Sociology* (1895). Ironically, Thoreau was not around to see one of the first formal sociology appointments in America, which was actually held by one of Ralph Waldo Emerson's descendants: Samuel Franklin Emerson began his post as professor of history and sociology at the University of Vermont in 1889. However, Thoreau certainly did witness the beginning of a social science movement in the United States, and was doing some of his most important writing as the ideas of social thinkers such as Comte and Spencer were gaining influence in American social thought. And while Thoreau saw his own project as broader than developing a science of society, his work certainly demonstrates that he shared similar aims with important figures in the history of sociology who came before and after him, and that he was on the forefront of a perspective that would later develop into an entire formal academic discipline.

Thoreau's Political Legacy

In addition to the objectives he shared with other critical social thinkers such as Jane Addams, W. E. B. Du Bois, and C. Wright Mills, there stands another reason for examining Thoreau as a social thinker: his legacy of social change. Thoreau's ideas have profoundly impacted public discussion and views on nature and the environment, individuality, the conscience of the citizen, dissent, simplicity, and self-cultivation. He has been associated with a number of major social movements, including environmentalism, "voluntary simplicity," nineteenth-century abolition, and twentieth-century civil rights. In fact, he has posthumously been adopted as an icon into the camps of a countless "pro" or "anti" activist groups—antiwar, pro-green, antiauthority, prosimplicity, antigovernment, proindividuality, and antimaterialism. He has been cited as an important influence on numerous figures, including Gandhi, Martin Luther King Jr., W. E. B. Du Bois, Leo Tolstoy, B. F. Skinner, the sociologist David Riesman (author of The Lonely Crowd), and Benton McKaye, an environmental philosopher who started the Appalachian Trail.[62] Thoreauvian works such as Walden and "Civil Disobedience" have been used as manuals for radical political reform in India, South Africa, Bulgaria, Denmark, and the Netherlands.[63] From protesting the Nazis to battling colonial rule, Thoreau's message has been invoked to mobilize resistance to injustice. During the twentieth century, Walden was translated into every major language. Thoreau's works, including "Civil Disobedience," remain popular, particularly in countries where his work has played an important role in social change.

Because of the powerful message in his writing, reaction to Thoreau from official organizations has been mixed. In India the government actually sponsored the translation of Walden into fifteen of the country's major languages, and the United States government has also sponsored translations.[64] However, in the 1950s Senator Joseph McCarthy was successful in removing books from United States Information Service libraries around the world because they contained Thoreau's "Civil Disobedience."[65] Thoreau also left his imprint on academia. His ideas are used in economic and political theory, natural history, environmental studies and ecology, and literature. Walden is not only regarded as a masterpiece of American literature, but also a cultural icon of the environmental movement.[66] Few social theorists have had such reach.

Thoreau's influence on Gandhi and King requires special attention, given the global association of all three figures with political resistance and civil disobedience. Gandhi was introduced to Thoreau's works by the English educator Henry Salt, who wrote one of the first biographies of Thoreau and worked to popularize him outside the United States. Salt and Gandhi were vegetarians, and met in England when Gandhi had come there to study law in the late 1880s.[67] Thoreau's work became more meaningful and important to Gandhi when he led protests in Johannesburg, South Africa, against the

Asiatic Law Amendment Ordinance, which became effective on July 1, 1907. Also known as the "Black Act," the law required all Indians in South Africa over the age of eight to be fingerprinted and to carry a certificate of registration with them at all times. Any Indian who failed to register could be fined, put in jail, or deported. In Johannesburg, Gandhi helped to found the Passive Resistance Association, later called "Satyagraha Association," which protested the law. Unhappy with the words "passive resistance," he later chose an Indian word, "Satyagraha," which means the force born of truth, love, and nonviolence. Shortly after the law was enacted Gandhi was arrested, fined, and imprisoned for his part in organizing demonstrations. The government later decided to make the registration voluntary, and Gandhi was released from prison. However, when the government went back on their promise, he was arrested again after leading a protest in which thousands of Indians burned registration cards. During this jail term, while in the Volksrust Prison, he read "Civil Disobedience" for the first time. "It left a deep impression on me," Gandhi stated.[68] By this time, he had already read *Walden*:

> I read Walden first in Johannesburg in South Africa in 1906, and his ideas influenced me greatly. I adopted some of them and recommended the study of Thoreau to all my friends who were helping me in the cause of Indian independence. . . . There is no doubt that Thoreau's ideas greatly influenced my movement in India.[69]

Gandhi's movement in South Africa was successful enough that he eventually returned to India to lead an independence movement against the British for "home rule." Through the use of marches, boycotts, and labor strikes, Gandhi led the nation of India in a protest against British colonial rule, which included physical mistreatment of Indians as well as economic exploitation of Indian workers and natural resources. The protesters, Gandhi demanded, were not to respond with physical force, even when brutally attacked by the British. He took Thoreau's title, "Civil Disobedience," as an English translation for this movement. He states in *Non-violent Resistance* (1961) that until he "read that essay I never found a suitable English translation for my Indian word, *Satyagraha*."[70] However, he later changed the English name of the movement to "Civil Resistance."

Gandhi became known globally for the nonviolent protests that thwarted and wore down the British Empire, especially when India won its freedom from the British (1947). Widespread interest in Gandhi's biography and spiritual life led followers, journalists, and the public to focus on his appreciation of Thoreau's work.[71] Many were surprised to find that there are significant differences between the two figures: for example, Thoreau's reform focused on the individual rather than society, while Gandhi was interested in motivating the masses in India. More importantly, while Gandhi vehemently held to nonviolence as a strategy, Thoreau evolved to an acceptance of violence as a means of social reform. Despite these differences, though, it is clear from Gandhi's own words that Thoreau's work had a tremendous effect on him. While in jail Gandhi took comfort and inspiration from Thoreau's words, and both men romanticized the jail cell as a place where the individual's soul was free. *Walden* influenced Gandhi's disillusionment with modernization and technology, particularly with respect to the effects that "civilization" and the "West" had on Colonial India.[72] Like Thoreau, Gandhi was skeptical of the moral benefits of the complex division of labor that Britain brought to India. In fact, Gandhi's movement for Indians to use "homespun" fabric, made by hand rather than bought from British plunderers, parallels Thoreau's efforts toward self-reliance. Gandhi was also attracted to the Thoreauvian ideas of "action from principle" and "simplicity." Although he was practicing civil disobedience before he read Thoreau's essay, Gandhi was quick to point out the debt he owed to Thoreau and other thinkers like him. In the preface of "Hind Swaraj" in the *Indian Opinion*, he states, "While the views expressed in the Hind Swaraj are held by me, I have only endeavored to humbly to follow Tolstoy, Ruskin, Thoreau, Emerson and other writers, besides the masters of Indian philosophy."[73]

Dr. Martin Luther King Jr. first encountered Thoreau while he was a fifteen-year-old sociology major at Morehouse College. In his autobiography he states:

> During my student days I read Henry David Thoreau's essay "On Civil Disobedience" for the first time. Here, in the courageous New Englander's refusal to pay his taxes and his choice of jail rather than support a war that would spread slavery's territory into Mexico, I made my first contact with the theory of non-violent resistance. Fascinated by the idea of refusing to cooperate with an evil system, I was so deeply moved that I reread the work several times.[74]

After completing the residential requirements for a PhD from Boston University at age twenty-five, King became the pastor of the historic Dexter Avenue Baptist Church of Montgomery, Alabama. Less than a year later, on December 1, 1955, Rosa Parks was arrested for violating segregation laws by refusing to give up her seat on a bus to a white passenger. In much of the South at that time black passengers were prohibited from sitting in reserved seats and were asked to vacate nonreserved seats when white passengers wanted them. Refusal to comply resulted in arrest. Within a day of Parks's arrest, plans for the historic Montgomery bus boycott had begun. The first day of the boycott, December 5, was an overwhelming success, and that evening King was elected as the president of the newly formed Montgomery Improvement Association. In his autobiography King reflects on the similarities between the ideas Thoreau wrote about in "Civil Disobedience" and the objectives of the civil rights movement:

> [T]he basic aim was to refuse to cooperate with an evil system. At this point I began to think about Thoreau's "Essay on Civil Disobedience." I became convinced that what we were preparing to do in Montgomery was related to what Thoreau had expressed. We were simply saying to the white community, "We can no longer lend our cooperation to an evil system." From this moment on I conceived of our movement as an act of massive non-cooperation.[75]

King expanded this noncooperation movement throughout the South and to other parts of the United States, including Chicago and Los Angeles. Just as Gandhi did before him, King used sit-ins at lunch counters, demonstration marches, and economic boycotts to advocate for voting rights and integration in schools, restaurants, and other public places. Like Thoreau and Gandhi, King spent his share of time in jail. He was arrested more than twenty times for such crimes as "speeding," leading an "illegal" boycott, and "failing to obey an officer." Just as Thoreau's night in jail inspired him to write "Civil Disobedience," King's stay in the Birmingham jail prompted him to write one of his most moving and famous essays, "Letter from a Birmingham Jail." King was arrested on April 12, 1963, for violating a state circuit court injunction against protests, and was eventually placed in solitary confinement. That same day several white Birmingham ministers had taken an ad out in the newspaper calling for an end to the demonstrations. King began writing his response on the margins of the newspaper, and finished it on scraps of paper and a legal pad he eventually obtained from his lawyer. "Letter from a Birmingham Jail" was King's staunch defense of his campaign, including the philosophy behind his nonviolent protests and noncooperation, as well as an examination of just and unjust laws. Like "Civil Disobedience," King's "Letter" remains not only a powerful call to action aimed at the conscience of every American citizen, but also one of the most important political essays in the history of the United States.

King, like Gandhi, differed from Thoreau on several significant issues related to reform. For example, King saw the government as an institution that would have a role in reorganizing society. Thoreau believed reform began with the individual, not with institutions. King, like Gandhi, held to the concept of nonviolence until his death. Toward the end of his life, Thoreau defended the militant abolitionist John Brown as an American hero. Despite these differences, though, in his autobiography King clearly pays homage to Thoreau's influence on the civil rights movement:

> I became convinced that non-cooperation with evil is as much a moral obligation as is cooperation with good. No other person has been more eloquent and passionate in getting this idea across than Henry David Thoreau. As a result of his writings and personal witness, we are the heirs of a legacy of creative protest. The teachings of Thoreau came alive in our civil rights movement; indeed, they are more alive than every before. Whether expressed in a sit-in at lunch counters, a freedom-ride into Mississippi, a peaceful protest in Albany, Georgia, a bus boycott in Montgomery, Alabama, these are the outgrowths of Thoreau's insistence that evil must be resisted and that no moral man can patiently adjust to injustice.[76]

From his surrounding influences to his intellectual lineage, his mission to his legacy, Thoreau shares common ground with other social theorists and with the field of sociology. Although his critique of modernity, including capitalism, parallels other social theorists, including Karl Marx, few theorists have attempted to cover such a range of issues, and few have had as broad an audience as Thoreau. He uniquely synthesized the ideas of the Enlightenment and Romantic movements in an effort to explore such issues as the effects of society on the individual, the characteristics of "natural man," and the relationship between nature and civilization. While he has primarily been recognized as a literary master, Thoreau's ideas have extended beyond academic fields such as political philosophy to play an important role in social reform. He has been a voice for the environment and for dissent. His legacy embodies all that early social theorists such as Comte hoped that in-depth analysis of society would yield. Yet I have presented here only the roots and fruits of Thoreau's work. An in-depth examination of his social analysis is the best way to understand Thoreau's sociological imagination. This will begin in the following chapter with an exploration of his ideas on how structures of society, such as the economy and government, affect the individual.

Notes

1. For a concise but thorough biography of Thoreau, see William Cain's "Henry David Thoreau 1817–1862: A Brief Biography," in *A Historical Guide to Henry David*

Thoreau, ed. William Cain, 11–57 (New York: Oxford University Press, 2000). For a more in-depth biography and intellectual history of Thoreau, see Robert D. Richardson Jr.'s *Henry Thoreau: A Life of the Mind* (Berkeley and Los Angeles: University of California Press, 1986).

2. Richardson, *Henry Thoreau*, 8; Cain, "A Brief Biography."

3. Henry David Thoreau, "Walden," in *The Portable Thoreau*, rev. ed., ed. Carl Bode (New York: Penguin, 1987), 343.

4. Henry David Thoreau, *Journal 5: 1852–1853*, ed. Patrick O'Connell (Princeton, NJ: Princeton University Press, 1997), 549.

5. Richardson, *Henry Thoreau*, 105.

6. Richardson, *Henry Thoreau*, 166–69.

7. Richardson, *Henry Thoreau*, 381; Laura Dassow Walls, *Seeing New Worlds: Henry David Thoreau and Nineteenth-Century Natural Science* (Madison: University of Wisconsin Press, 1995), 3–14.

8. Irving Zeitlin, *Ideology and the Development of Sociological Theory*, 6th ed. (Upper Saddle River, NJ: Prentice-Hall, 1997), 2.

9. Zeitlin, *Ideology and the Development of Sociological Theory*, 3.

10. Zeitlin, *Ideology and the Development of Sociological Theory*, 6.

11. For easy-to-access online discussions of Transcendentalism see Michael Frederick's "Transcendental Ethos: A Study of Thoreau's Social Philosophy and Its Consistency in Relation to Antebellum Reform" (MA thesis, Harvard University, 1998), thoreau.eserver.org/MJF/MJF.html (accessed May 12, 2002) and Paul Rueben's "American Transcendentalism: A Brief Introduction," chap. 4 in *PAL: Perspectives on American Literature: A Research and Reference Guide*, web.csustan.edu/english/reuben/pal/chap4/4intro.html (accessed May 13, 2002).

12. Rueben, "American Transcendentalism: A Brief Introduction."

13. Robert Lawrence France, "Introduction," in *Thoreau on Water: Reflecting Heaven*, ed. Robert France, xix–xxi (Boston: Mariner, 2001).

14. John Rice, "Romantic Modernism and the Self," *Hedgehog Review* 1 (Fall 1999), www.virginia.edu/iasc/hh/THRtoc1–1.html (accessed January 1, 2007), 2.

15. Rice, "Romantic Modernism and the Self," 2.

16. Richardson, *Henry Thoreau*, 74.

17. Emerson, Thoreau, and Frederick Douglass wrote and spoke on issues such as slavery, education and, commerce. Other Transcendentalist members such as Nathaniel Hawthorne and Walt Whitman also injected political and moral imperatives into their literature.

18. See Leslie Wilson's "New England Transcendentalism," *Concord* (November 1993), www.concordma.com/magazine/nov98/trans.html (accessed May 14, 2002).

19. Richardson, *Henry Thoreau*, 73.

20. Wendell Glick, "Henry David Thoreau (1817–1862)," in *The Heath Anthology of American Literature*, 3rd ed., ed. P Lauter, 1964–2062 (Lexington, MA: D. C. Heath, 1990).

21. Paul Rueben, "Romanticism—A Brief Introduction," chap. 3 in *PAL: Perspectives on American Literature: A Research and Reference Guide.* web.csustan.edu/english/reuben/pal/chap3/3intro.html (accessed May 13, 2002).

22. Thomas Hampson, "Romanticism," in *I Hear America Singing*, 1997, www.pbs.org/wnet/ihas/icon/romanticism.html (accessed May 14, 2002).

23. Zeitlin, *Ideology and the Development of Sociological Theory*, 48.

24. Zeitlin, *Ideology and the Development of Sociological Theory*, 47.

25. Richardson, *Henry Thoreau*, 72–73.

26. Zeitlin, *Ideology and the Development of Sociological Theory*, 18–24.

27. Zeitlin, *Ideology and the Development of Sociological Theory*, 19.

28. Zeitlin, *Ideology and the Development of Sociological Theory*, 18.

29. Zeitlin, *Ideology and the Development of Sociological Theory*, 46.

30. France, "Introduction," xix.

31. Lawrence Buell, "Thoreau and the Natural Environment," in *The Cambridge Companion to Henry David Thoreau*, ed. Joel Myerson (New York: Cambridge University Press, 1995), 171; France, "Introduction," xix.

32. It was civil society, according to both thinkers, that gave rise to problems. See M. A. Glendon's "Rousseau and the Revolt against Reason," *First Things* 96 (October 1999): 42–47, and Zeitlin, *Ideology and the Development of Sociological Theory*, 18–22.

33. Thoreau, *Journal 5*, 511.

34. Richardson, *Henry Thoreau*, 32–33.

35. Thoreau, "Walden," 286–87.

36. Lewis Hyde, "Introduction: Prophetic Excursions," in *The Essays of Henry David Thoreau*, ed. Lewis Hyde, vii–li (New York: North Point Press, 2002).

37. Richardson, *Henry Thoreau*, 167.

38. Richardson, *Henry Thoreau*, 167.

39. Richardson, *Henry Thoreau*, 168–69.

40. Brian Walker, "Thoreau's Alterative Economics: Work, Liberty, Democratic Cultivation," *American Political Science Review* 92, no. 4 (1998): 847.

41. Walker, "Thoreau's Alternative Economics," 848.

42. See Nancy Baym, "Thoreau's View of Science," *Journal of the History of Ideas* 26 (1965): 221–34, and Elizabeth Witherell and Elizabeth Dubrulle, "The Life and Times of Henry D. Thoreau," *The Writings of Henry D. Thoreau*, 1999, libws66.lib.niu.edu/thoreau/thoreau.htm (accessed June 27, 2000).

43. See Baym, "Thoreau's View of Science"; and Walls, "Seeing New Worlds."

44. Henry David Thoreau, *Journal 3: 1848–1851*, ed. Robert Sattelmeyer, Mark Patterson, and William Rossi (Princeton, NJ: Princeton University Press, 1990), 353.

45. Walls, "Seeing New Worlds," 3–14.

46. Walls, "Seeing New Worlds," 11.

47. Henry David Thoreau, *The Journal of Henry David Thoreau*, ed. Bradford Torrey and Francis Allen (Boston: Houghton Mifflin, 1906), XIII: 77–78.

48. Walls, "Seeing New Worlds," 6.

49. See Baym, "Thoreau's View of Science"; and Walls, "Seeing New Worlds."

50. Richardson, *Henry Thoreau*, 223.

51. L. L. Bernard and Jessie Bernard, *The Origins of American Sociology: The Social Science Movement in the United States* (New York: Russell and Russell, 1965), 59–69.

52. Lance Newman, "Thoreau's Natural Community and Utopian Socialism," *American Literature* 75, no. 3 (2003): 524.

53. Newman, "Thoreau's Natural Community and Utopian Socialism," 537.

54. Richardson, *Henry Thoreau*, 376.

55. Richardson, *Henry Thoreau*, 369.

56. Richardson, *Henry Thoreau*, 330–31.

57. Bernard and Bernard, *The Origins of American Sociology*, 130.

58. Bernard and Bernard, *The Origins of American Sociology*, 131.

59. Bernard and Bernard, *The Origins of American Sociology*, 135.

60. Bernard and Bernard, *The Origins of American Sociology*, 141.

61. George Ritzer, *Classical Sociological Theory*, 3rd ed. (Boston: McGraw-Hill, 2000), 147.

62. Sherman Paul, "Introduction," in *Thoreau: A Collection of Critical Essays*, ed. Sherman Paul (Englewood Cliffs, NJ: Prentice-Hall, 1962), 2.

63. See Paul, "Introduction," 1–7; Walter Harding, "Thoreau's Reputation," in *The Cambridge Companion to Henry David Thoreau*, ed. Joel Myerson (New York: Cambridge University Press, 1995), 1–11; Albena Bakratcheva, "Henry David Thoreau and the Spiritual Emancipation in Bulgaria" (paper presented at the Annual Thoreau Society Meeting, Concord, MA, 1993), LiterNet.revolta.com/publish/alba/texts/_fulb-st.htm (accessed May 10, 2002).

64. Harding, "Thoreau's Reputation," 9.

65. Walter Harding, *Variorum Civil Disobedience* (New York: Irvington Publications, 1968), 10.

66. Lawrence Buell, *The Environmental Imagination: Thoreau, Nature Writing and the Formation of American Culture* (Cambridge, MA: Belknap Press of Harvard University Press, 1995), 313–16.

67. Harding, "Thoreau's Reputation," 7.

68. Henry Salt, "Gandhi and Thoreau," *Nation and Athenaeum*, 46, no. 22 (1930): 728.

69. Yogesh Chadha, *Gandhi: A Life.* (New York: John Wiley and Sons, 1999), 138.

70. Mohandas Gandhi, *Non-violent Resistance*, ed. Bharatan Kumarappa (New York: Schocken Books, 1961), 14.

71. See Chadha's *Gandhi* for a more in-depth discussion of the public interest in Gandhi's ideas on Thoreau.

72. Chadha, *Gandhi*, 159.

73. Mohandas Gandhi, "Hind Swaraj or Indian Home Rule," *Indian Opinion*, December 11 and 18, 1909: 2.

74. Martin Luther King Jr., *The Autobiography of Martin Luther King, Jr.*, ed. Clayborne Carson (New York: Time Warner, 1998), 14.

75. King, *Autobiography*, 54.

76. King, *Autobiography*, 14.

CHAPTER THREE

~

Social Structures and the American Individual

The mass of men lead lives of quiet desperation. What is called resignation is confirmed desperation. . . . A stereotyped but unconscious despair is concealed even under what are called the games and amusements of mankind. There is no play in them, for this comes only after work.[1]

But lo! men have become the tools of their tools.[2]

If the laborer gets no more than the wages which his employer pays him, he is cheated, he cheats himself. . . . You are paid for being something less than a man.[3]

Thoreau, like other social theorists, examined various structures and components of society, including the economy, government, slavery, education, the social class system, and the American public. Yet he was primarily concerned with exploring the ways in which these social structures and institutions actually shaped the life of the individual. One of the most recurring topics of Thoreau's writings was his examination of how the economic system of his time increasingly structured daily life. The evolving industrial capitalist system, he argued, was not only affecting the workplace and workday, but also the human experience of time, leisure, and nature. The changes in social values that accompanied capitalism—including an intense focus on accumulating material goods, new social definitions of "progress," and the transfer of time into a commodity—meant that Americans spent less time on self-examination and the development of human relationships. The result, Thoreau argued, was an economic system that infringed on individual freedom and often enslaved the individual conscience by instilling anxiety, alienation, and despair. The ethos of capitalism transformed time, nature, and humans into objects and market commodities. In addition to his critique of the American economic system, Thoreau also spent a great deal of his writing scrutinizing the role of the American government as a dominant social institution. Much of his work, such as "Civil Disobedience," and "Slavery in Massachusetts," contains ideas on how the political system trampled on individual liberty. The utilitarian, or, as Thoreau referred to it, "expedient," government often imposed its will on the individual conscience. The combination of these two influential social structures on the American people created a public ethos that was not only complacent in the face of injustice, but also more concerned with commerce than liberty. For Thoreau, these issues were not simply academic. He saw the effects of these social structures on individual life as a significant social problem. Most of his writings, including *Walden* and "Life without Principle," were an effort to solve these problems of daily life created by the effects of broader social structures on the individual.

The Economy and the Individual

Thoreau begins his essay "Life without Principle" with a call to consider "the way we spend our lives," and he argues that that there has been little "written on the subject of getting a living."[4] This was a timely issue for Thoreau—he saw his world as a place of nonstop work and industry, which created an obstacle to the more important matters of life, such as self-development:

> The world is a place of business. What an infinite bustle! I am awakened almost every night by the panting of the locomotive. . . . [T]here is no Sabbath. It would be great to see mankind at leisure for once. It is nothing but work, work, work. I cannot easily buy a blank-book to write my thoughts in; they are commonly ruled for dollars and cents. . . . I think there is nothing, not even crime, more opposed to poetry, to philosophy, to life itself, than this incessant business.[5]

Thoreau's primary critique of the market system was that it functioned as a place of servility and humiliation—of the individual conscience and of life itself.[6] He believed that the widespread fixation on work ethic, which drove modern capitalism, extinguished human dignity.

Workers, he argued, squandered the best parts of their humanity in return for trivial concerns and anxieties over luxury items and public opinion. As consumers, Americans became more preoccupied with superfluous activities, while their work lives transformed them into nothing more than animals or machines. However, the economic system did not simply alienate humans from their own selves by limiting self-development and devaluing the individual conscience; it also alienated people from each other by creating so many preoccupations and concerns with the marketplace that there was little time for developing true social relationships. In Thoreau's view, the overall effect of this American economic system was a complete objectification and invalidation of human life. Workers and consumers actually became objects in the market system, which was contrary to the subjective experience of life that he and the rest of the Transcendentalists were seeking.

The Capitalist Clock

While Thoreau, as a Transcendentalist, sought a more subjective, nonconventional, and nonlinear lifestyle, eighteenth-century capitalism was increasingly structuring the ways humans experienced time.[7] The economy was not simply determining how people were "getting a living" and spending their money, but also how they were spending each hour of the day. Rather than the Transcendentalist ideal of subjective experience, industrial capitalism had transformed time into a commodity—a new form of capital.[8] As a result, work and leisure time became more structured. Thoreau feared that the new cost-benefit measurement of time would result in more time spent at work and less time spent on self-development and self-reflective activities. The whole "village day," he argues in *Walden*, was increasingly being structured by the temporal agents of capitalism:

> The startings and arrivals of the cars are now the epochs in the village day. They go and come with such regularity and precision, and their whistle can be heard so far, that the farmers set their clocks by them, and thus one well conducted institution regulates a whole country. Have not men improved somewhat in punctuality since the railroad was invented? Do they not talk and think faster in the depot than they did in the stage-office? . . . To do things "railroad fashion" is now the by-word. . . . We have constructed a fate, an *Atropos*, that never turns aside.[9]

James Guthrie, who has written extensively on Thoreau's view of time, points out that throughout his life Thoreau was actually seeking a reform of structured time, especially the commodification of it.[10] Thoreau believed the human construct of time had no equivalent in nature. In his emphasis on experiencing the present moment, he drew a distinction between the capitalist construction of time and time experienced naturally.[11] Thoreau did this, in part, by pointing out the illusions of the capitalist incentive system in regards to time. Many workers were motivated by the logic that the more money they had, the more free time they would possess. Thoreau argued that this was incorrect. Humans had less free time than ever, despite having more luxuries. An urgency to accumulate more material goods exaggerated this problem. The more debt people accrued by purchasing goods, Thoreau argued, the more their time was owed to someone else.[12] Likewise, the larger the home or farm that one owned, the more time was required for upkeep. To resist the absolute commandeering of time by industrial capitalism, Thoreau aimed, through experiments such as his extended stay at Walden, to wrestle back the subjective splendor of time for the individual.

In his effort to transcend a capitalist model of time, Thoreau looked beyond conventional American society for advice. Human relations, he argued, were more authentic in nature, where the hasty, temporal pressures of capitalism could not wield power over the dynamics of human interaction.[13] Outside of the realms of the market system, humans could be on "event time," rather than "clock time," which allowed for more authentic human relationships.[14] Thoreau pointed to his own experiment at Walden to demonstrate the possibilities for human relationships when conventional ideas of time had been transcended: "I had more visitors while I lived in the woods than at any other period in my life; I mean that I had some. I met several there under more favorable circumstances than I could anywhere else. But fewer came to see me on trivial business."[15] Thoreau also examined how different cultures experience time, constructing a model of temporal differences between the "Occidental" and the "Oriental" in A Week on the Concord and Merrimack Rivers.[16] An Occidental experience of time was like that of industrial American, hurried and full of activity. The Oriental experience of time involved more contemplation. Those with an Oriental view of time operate where time is not operative, sleeping when the rest of the world is bustling and active when this bustling "sets." To Thoreau, these individuals had transcended conventional time. This ability to transcend the hold and structure that conventional time enacted on individuals was essential, he believed, for a more authentic and natural existence.[17]

Capitalist Values

While the activities of the day became more structured by the economy, so too did the values and "needs" of the day. Thoreau observed that much of the population bought in to the ethos under which capitalism functioned, which resulted in increased materialism and the pretentiousness of the American social class system. These values had become the sacred "truth" by which most lived their lives.[18] Individuals and their activities were judged by their proximity and value to the market. With an increased emphasis on status, those with less desirable clothing or less worthy careers were themselves deemed less desirable and less worthy. External attributes and behavior—such as clothing or career—became symbols used by Americans to assess internal characteristics such as individual character. Thoreau portrayed concrete examples of these truths by examining how material items were given social value or how goods became fetishized.

In particular, he looked at social ideas about clothing to demonstrate this process. He first considered the basic utility of clothing and how, with the capitalist ethos, the "need" for clothing evolved into something altogether different. In this materialistic culture, consumer behavior was not driven by utility or need but by a desire to be "fashionable." Poignantly, Thoreau even pondered how we might determine people's social class rank if they were divested of their clothing.[19] This use of clothing to signify status, he believed, demonstrated the widespread fetishism of material goods. Capitalist ethos not only structured the primary motives of consumer behavior but also instilled anxiety over one's social standing. In *Walden*, for example, Thoreau states:

> As for clothing, to come at once to the practical part of the question, perhaps we are left oftener by love of novelty and a regard for the opinions of men, in procuring it, than by true utility. . . .
> . . . No man ever stood the lower in my estimation for having a patch on his clothes; yet I am sure that there is a greater anxiety, commonly, to have fashionable, or at least clean and unpatched clothes, than to have a sound conscience. . . . I sometimes try my acquaintances by such tests as this- who could wear a patch, or two extra seams only, over the knee? Most behave as if they believed their prospects for life would be ruined if they should do it. It would be easier for them to hobble to town with a broken leg than with a broken pantaloon.[20]

The effects of these new social values on consumer behavior were clear to Thoreau—decisions about which clothes to purchase or wear were based on public opinion, novelty, and fashion, rather than utility. Anxiety and scrutiny over clothing trumped more important matters, such as tending to one's conscience. As the individual and public conscience became preoccupied with fashion, Americans even began to believe that their "prospects for life" could be damaged simply by their clothing choices. In the lives of many Americans, Thoreau pointed out, what to wear had become a crisis.[21]

Though he disdained it, Thoreau recognized that fashion anxiety and an obsession with the newest trends held authority as a powerful social force that structured public consumption. For example, in *Walden* Thoreau describes an incident where he had requested a particular form of clothing, but his seamstress informed him that "they" do not make such clothing anymore.[22] Thoreau continues in this passage to question who "they" were and why "they" should exercise authority over what he should wear. He even equates the conformity of fashion to monkeys in America mimicking monkeys in France. However, Thoreau knew that the markets were not strictly governed by structured authoritarian dictates: There was not simply a "they" who prescribe market behavior, as Thoreau's seamstress suggested; rather, consumer behavior within the market and public opinion toward particular products were often whimsical, leaving the manufacturers clamoring to figure out the most desired and contemporary fashions. Two clothing patterns may differ by only a few threads, Thoreau points out, but one will sell widely, while the other sits on the shelf.[23] Yet, even though these new artificial needs were fabricated and arbitrary, consumer anxiety and scrutiny over clothing increasingly trumped more important matters.

Thoreau also recognized that the capitalist value system determined which activities, and, by association, which individuals, were characterized as valuable, industrious, efficient, or lazy. He addresses this topic in detail in the essay "Life without Principle," where he argues that if he chose to engage in the "real labors which yield more profit" by walking through the woods, he would be regarded as a loafer.[24] Yet if he were to work as a speculator who clear-cut the woods for profit, he would be seen as industrious and enterprising. Indeed, he pointed out that most people sought out his company not for the purpose of a meaningful relationship, but because they desired his services as a surveyor or because they were interested in the trivial news of the day.[25] Thoreau understood that humans were increasingly valued in society because of the utility of their physical body and their contributions to the market. At one point in "Life without Principle," he laments that if an infant were to become incapacitated for life, it would be regretted by society because of the loss to the market of a consumer and a worker.[26] In *Walden* he explores how the ethos of materialism was so strong that it often usurped life itself, including the sad event of a man's death. He recounts how the death of a local resident brought people out to pawn through his belongings rather than to mourn his death.[27] The scene Thoreau depicts is analogous to animals scavenging a carcass. Not even in the event of the death of an acquaintance did the public's materialism cease. Though a life had ended, the life of the consumer goods did not—materialism had outlived the individual.

The Marketing of Nature
The economy was also encroaching on another of Thoreau's sacred arenas—nature. As Lawrence Buell, author of *The Environmental Imagination* (1995), points out, Thoreau was the only major American writer to have made a living from surveying tracts of land, which gave him a command of geography.[28] This practical view of nature, along with his spiritual understanding of nature, led him to believe that the current economic structure alienated humans from nature in several ways. The economy was increasingly marketing nature, emptying it of its spiritual meaning and ruining its purity. The increasing economic interest in development and raw materials led to the physical invasion and destruction of nature.[29] A number of Thoreau's works address the marketing of nature by the American economic system, including *Walden*, *Journal*, and *The Maine Woods*. For example, in *Walden* he writes about how industry was "penetrating" the realm of nature and processing its fruits for profit:

> The whistle of the locomotive penetrates my woods summer and winter, sounding like the scream of a hawk sailing over some farmer's yard, informing me that many restless city merchants are arriving within the circle of the town, or adventurous country traders from the other side. . . . [T]imber like long battering rams going twenty miles an hour against the city's walls . . . Indian huckleberry hills are stripped, all the cranberry meadows are raked into the city; up comes the silk, down goes the woolen; up come the books, but down goes the wit that writes them.[30]

To Thoreau "wealth" meant "spiritual purity, simplicity, and leisure," and Walden was an ideal place for that "business."[31] Nature itself was meant to be a place of reflection and self-cultivation: "A lake is the landscape's most beautiful and expressive feature. It is earth's eye; looking into which the beholder measures the depth of his own nature."[32] It was also meant to be a place of purity—Thoreau argues in *Walden* that the pond was too pure to have a market value.[33] Yet capitalism had developed a vastly different use for nature. Thoreau was troubled by industry's encroachment into his "holy nature," which profaned it and drained it of its spiritual meaning.[34] Sacred natural objects such as land or water were turned into an investment, while the simple farmer was transformed into a businessman. Instead of going to the pond to drink, its waters were brought to the village through a pipe to wash the dishes.

The railroad, or "Iron Horse," had brought deforestation and pollution to the waters of Walden Pond.[35] Capitalism, Thoreau argued, had seized on the wilderness, absconded with its raw materials back to the city, and transformed its fruits into a commodity.

In *Walden* Thoreau discusses his disdain for this transformation process in a number of ways, including his descriptions of an entrepreneur of agriculture, the removal of ice from Walden Pond for commercial purposes, and the transport and marketing of huckleberries. Flint, the agricultural entrepreneur, is introduced by Thoreau in the chapter of *Walden* entitled "The Ponds." Thoreau describes him as a crafty capitalist—everything had a price on his farm. Flint's fields were not ripe until they were "turned into dollars."[36] The farmer would even "carry his God, to market" if he knew it would bring financial gain.[37] This strict entrepreneurial approach to agriculture focused solely on its exchange value and altered the very essence of the natural objects.[38] Later in *Walden*, Thoreau recounts the removal of ice from Walden Pond. He describes the arrival of a hundred men with sleds, drill-barrows, turf-knives, spades, saws and pike-staffs who came in the winter of 1846 to 1847 to extract the ice.[39] Yet he clearly points out that this was not the purpose for which nature intended the lake. Whereas the lake was meant to be an object of reflection, purity, and solitude, these properties were ignored by the workers. The exchange process of the market had emptied these most important aspects of nature, and structured the pond as an arena of work. Likewise, in his description of the transport and marketing of huckleberries on their way to Boston, Thoreau explains the change that the fruit underwent:

> The fruits do not yield their true flavor to the purchaser of them, nor to him who raises them for the market. . . . It is a vulgar error to suppose that you have tasted huckleberries who have never plucked them. A huckleberry never reaches Boston . . . . The ambrosial and essential part of the fruit is lost with the bloom that is rubbed off in the market cart, and they become mere provender. As long as Eternal Justice reigns, not one innocent huckleberry can be transported thither from the country's hills.[40]

The "wildness" and truest essence of the fruit was profaned in the exchange process. Widespread deforestation not only deformed the landscape, it also made the wilderness "tame and cheap," because humans could not read fully into its meaning.[41] The purity and spiritual utility of nature became depleted by the exchange process of industry and capitalism's unnatural definitions of value and utility.

Economy and the Physical Destruction of Nature
In addition to the transformation of the spiritual aspects of nature, Thoreau
was also concerned with its physical destruction. He was aware of the exter-
mination of animals and recognized conservation as a public issue.[42] In his
writing Thoreau notes a spectrum of imprints that humans had left in the
wilderness. In "Ktaadn," a chapter of *The Maine Woods*, he responds to a less
extreme, yet still disconcerting, trace humans had left behind:

> But it was still startling to discover so plain a trail of civilized men there. I re-
> member that I was strangely affected when we were returning, by the sight of
> a ring-bolt well drilled into a rock, and fastened with lead, at the head of this
> solitary Ambejijis Lake.[43]

In *Walden* he explains the more intense effects of civilization on nature by
describing an observable change in the physical area around Walden Pond
since his arrival. The first time he paddled out onto the pond, it was surrounded by thick pines and oak. But after he left, the woodchoppers had "laid
them waste."[44] Some of the more extreme impacts Thoreau describes in his
works were a direct result of the logging industry. He observed the rapid expansion of the milling industry, which was altering the landscape of a number of areas that he visited in Massachusetts and Maine. He even spent time
visiting the loggers in several camps and mills, documenting the conditions
of work and the characteristics of the workers.[45] Such observations led
Thoreau to believe that the logging industry was responsible for the careless
destruction of entire forests by accidental fire, due to the fact that the area
itself was devalued after the pines were cut:

> The lumberers rarely trouble themselves to put their fires out, such is the
> dampness of the primitive forest; and this is one cause, no doubt, of the fre-
> quent fires in Maine, of which we hear so much on smoky days in Massa-
> chusetts. The forests are held cheap after the white pine has been culled
> out . . . [46]

In addition to the removal of trees, Thoreau also noted the effects of the
destruction on other aspects of the ecosystem, including animals. Many of his
descriptions in *Walden* include animal activity and animal characteristics. In
the *Walden* chapter "Winter Animals," for example, he discusses different
types of wildlife, including geese, owls, rabbits, grouse, mice, and even hunting dogs. He took great delight in watching and describing a number of animals found deep within nature. Such a physical and spiritual connection to

and appreciation of the natural world account for his discomfort with the in-
trusion of the economy into the forest:

> When I consider that the nobler animals have been exterminated here, the
> cougar, panther, lynx, wolverene, wolf, bear, moose, deer, the beaver, the
> turkey, etc., etc.,—I cannot but feel as if I lived in a tamed, and, as it were,
> emasculated country.[47]

Animals were as much a part of the wilderness as the vegetation, Thoreau believed, which meant that they were also an integral part of the spiritual community of the wilderness.[48] Yet human depreciation of wildlife was an emerging reality. Thoreau's uneasiness with this threat can be found throughout his
works and journals, but is certainly most recognized in *Walden*. For example,
in the in the chapter entitled "Brute Neighbors" he touches on over-hunting
by describing the hunting ratio as ten hunters to one loon. Sportsmen with
rifles are too often successful, he writes.[49] Later in *Walden* he describes the
sounds of the hunting hounds on the chase of wildlife. As the hunt ensued,
he writes, "man was in the rear," moving rapidly into nature's arena, while
animal and plant life suffered the consequences.[50]

Nature as Succor

Thoreau had a prophetic view of the physical and moral damage that could be
done if steps were not taken to promptly end the strict capitalist "exchange
value" perspective of natural resources. While some consider his work "shallow
ecology"—as "saving nature" for human endeavors—his interest in nature was
simultaneously poetic, philosophical, scientific, and spiritual. As both
Lawrence Buell and Richard Schneider point out, Thoreau's writings on nature
are both anthropocentric (human centered) and ecocentric.[51] For the purposes
of this book and chapter, however, I want to briefly focus on Thoreau's beliefs
about the benefits of nature to society, especially his concern for the relationship between humans and nature. Clearly, he was alarmed by the increasing
privatization of nature, which led him to question why America did not have
more national preserves and why we often poached our own national do-
mains.[52] "Walking," a lesser-known essay by Thoreau, is no less poignant than
Walden in challenging the view of land as a market commodity:

> At present, in this vicinity, the best part of the land is not private property; the
> landscape is not owned, and the walker enjoys comparative freedom. But pos-
> sibly the day will come when it will be partitioned off into so-called pleasure

grounds, in which a few will take a narrow and exclusive pleasure only,—when fences shall be multiplied, and man traps and other engines invented to confine men to the *public* road, and walking over the surface of God's earth shall be construed to mean trespassing on some gentleman's grounds. To enjoy a thing exclusively is commonly to exclude yourself from the true enjoyment of it. Let us improve our opportunities, then, before the evil days come.[53]

Thoreau aimed to demonstrate that the economy's infringement on nature—the traces left behind, fires, deforestation, over-hunting, and decrease of public land—functioned to decrease the individual's physical contact with the natural world. He wanted to "dismantle" the barriers between humans and nature.[54] The destruction of nature alienated humans from a proper and spiritually productive relationship with it. The very way in which humans could relate to the natural world was being altered by capitalism: "The explorers, and lumberers generally are all hirelings, paid so much a day for their labor, and as such, they have no more love for wild nature, than wood-sawyers have for forests."[55] This was quite different than Thoreau's ideal relationship in which humans were open to learning what nature had to teach. In reality, American society was taking a different route—humans were not "yielding" to nature's magnetism.[56]

This was partly due to the fact that in Thoreau's society the term "wilderness" was considered uncivilized, dirty, and even pagan—it was certainly not a place to seek spiritual clarity.[57] Thoreauvian works such as *Walden* and "Walking" were efforts to change this broadly held public conception of nature. Thoreau believed that America and even human civilization had much to gain from taking a wholly different view of nature and its utility. In nature, he argued, society could not only find more nourishment than in the materialism that the capitalist ethos was offering, but it could also find preservation. Nature would serve to "brace mankind" from many of its problems.[58] It offered society a physical encounter with goodness and strength. Thoreau argued that if society were willing to accept the succor that nature could provide through a proper relationship, the thoughts, ideas, and vision of America would improve. This would allow Americans to be more imaginative and to explore the inner depths of the individual mind.[59] Nature was a "tonic," but without the benefits of a relationship with it, humans became trapped in a limited world, unaware of their own potential and alienated from their own individual natural selves.

Comparing Thoreauvian and Marxian Social Analysis

In tone and judgment, Thoreau's view of capitalism seems proximate to that of Karl Marx. Thoreau and Marx were contemporaries, born a year apart.

Both men decried capitalism for its perversion of human nature, from the increased unnatural fixation on the accumulation of commodities to the increased alienation experienced by individuals. Coincidentally, perhaps, both men also lived in relative poverty most of their lives. Though they are both known for focusing on some of the same problems, there are three primary ways in which Thoreau and Marx differ: the starting point of their analyses of society, the explanations for why alienation occurs, and their solutions for liberating the individual.

Unlike Thoreau, Marx began his social analysis with the assumption that all aspects of human life—especially human consciousness—are determined by its material conditions. The economic base of society, Marx believed, influenced everything else, including cultural norms and the structure of the political system. This "materialist" assumption led Marx to explore one of the primary units of his social analysis, the relations of production within capitalism. He saw these relations as a struggle between workers (proletariat) and owners (bourgeoisie). Within capitalist societies, Marx pointed to the exploitation of laborers by owners as the primary conflict. Thoreau, on the other hand, put more emphasis on the intellectual and spiritual aspects of life, not the physical. Unlike Marx's "materialist" approach, Thoreau took an "idealist" perspective, focusing more on the conscious—rather than the physical—state of the individual. Thoreau did argue that the American economic system was negatively influencing people's lives, but he did not see the primary struggle as one between groups who have competing economic interests; rather, his focus was on the struggle between the individual and society. While Marx saw the owners as adversely shaping the lives of workers, Thoreau saw the manipulation of the individual conscience by society as the most pressing crisis needing resolution. Certainly Thoreau, like Marx, clearly recognized both the fetishism of fashion and the reification of the market.[60] There is no doubt that Thoreau was attuned to the ways in which Americans saw the marketplace and its values as "natural," a reality over which they had no control. Yet to Thoreau—the individualist—this situation was not a certain inevitability of the prevailing economic structure or of the physical conditions in which one lived:

> But men labor under a mistake. The better part of the man is soon ploughed into the soil for compost. By a seeming fate, commonly called necessity, they are employed . . . it is a fool's life.[61]

> Yet they honestly think there is no choice left. But alert and healthy natures remember that the sun rose clear. It is never too late to give up our prejudices.

No way of thinking or doing, however ancient, can be trusted without proof. What everybody echoes or in silence passes by as true to-day may turn out to be falsehood to-morrow, mere smoke of opinion, which some had trusted for a cloud that would sprinkle fertilizing rain on their fields. What old people say you cannot do, you try and find that you can. Old deeds for old people, and new deeds for new.[62]

The historian John Diggins is the only scholar to have written on the differences between Thoreau's and Marx's ideas on alienation and how each man believed it could be overcome.[63] Diggins points out that while both men viewed the alienation of humans from their natural state of being as an extremely problematic aspect of capitalism, they had different ideas about how it originated and how it could be conquered. For Marx, alienation originated from the way in which capitalism was structured, especially the unbalanced, exploitive relationship between the owners and the workers, and the organization of the mechanized factory system. The industrial workplace, Marx argued, transformed the work process from a creative activity into a mundane, repetitive endeavor where workers were powerless over the process. Workers were alienated from the products they produced as well as from the labor process itself. Marx was confident that alienation would end when the workers united in solidarity to reform the economic structure, transforming it from capitalism to communism.[64] Social action, in the form of a restructuring of the economic system, would allow the individual to once again experience a meaningful life by creatively expressing him- or herself in productive work. In other words, creative work would liberate workers from alienation.[65] Marx also believed that this type of cooperative action would bring out the collective nature of humanity and help individual workers to end their competition with each other in exchange for actualization with the larger community. He argued that a new social order was needed: one that inverted a world in which workers had little power, control, or choice.

Marx disdained individualism as a by-product of capitalism's self-interest ethos. He looked forward to a time when private property was abolished and humans worked as part of a collective group. Thoreau, however, saw individualism as a fundamental aspect of humanity. Indeed, Thoreau sought self-reliance, not collective or communal dependency on others. He believed that the individual should never have to acquiesce his or her will to the demands of a community. To Thoreau, alienation did not originate from the relations or modes of production or from an individual's inability to do creative productive work. He certainly did not share Marx's concerns for individual alienation from the labor process, or from the products themselves. Rather,

Thoreau saw alienation as the failure of the individual to engage in self-reflection and contemplation—the most important and meaningful enterprise for an individual's well-being. This often occurred when societal demands and social forces, such as the pressure to accumulate wealth, trumped the more important task of self-contemplation.

Finally, there are differences in how both men believed individual alienation could be overcome. Unlike Marx, Thoreau did not believe that creative productive work would solve the problem of alienation because it had several drawbacks.[66] First, it kept individuals from actively engaging in self-examination and contemplation. Second, productive work also typically involved human mastery and manipulation of nature. Both of these were cardinal sins to Thoreau. While Marx saw individual liberation resulting from communal social action that would allow workers to overthrow the economic system, reform for Thoreau began with the individual conscience—from the inside out.[67] It was a new individual that was needed, not necessarily a new social order. And though Thoreau did shift his views on reform to eventually accept that in some cases violence revolt was necessary—he supported and defended John Brown in his militant action against slavery—these cases typically involved reaction against a political state that imposed its will on the individual, not an overthrow of the predominant economic structure. Indeed Thoreau, unlike Marx, would never entrust social reform to a centralized state government that required individuals to consent their wills. For the most part Thoreau generally disliked social reformers and turned down offers to join reform-oriented communities such as Brook Farm. And unlike Marx's economic determinism, Thoreau argued that we already live in a world of our own choosing. In most cases if an individual wanted to end his or her own alienation, Thoreau believed, all that was needed was self-reflection and simplification, neither of which required any type of collective social action. Diggins characterizes the essence of the differences between Thoreau and Marx quite succinctly by pointing out that while Marx wanted to transform society, Thoreau sought to transcend it.[68]

The American Government

As much as Thoreau is recognized for his call to the American consumer to "simplify," and for his celebration of nature, some of his most widely read works also contain his ideas on government as a social institution. His treatise on the American government "Civil Disobedience," as well as *Walden* and the essay "Slavery in Massachusetts," explore the ways in which Thoreau believed the American government trampled on the individual conscience. These works were Thoreau's efforts to point out that American freedom was often an illusion—that there were obstacles built into the structure of the government that disempowered and devalued the individual. He explored several of these mechanisms within the government structure, including its expediency, the view of law as analogous to morality, the use of brute force to subdue dissent, and the abuse of power by elites. The utilitarian structure of the American government required that Americans resign their consciences to the will of legislators, effectively putting their duty as citizens above their obligation to the individual conscience. This left power in the hands of a few. An unquestioned faith in this system led the American public to equate morality with the "rule by majority" structure and legal codes such as the Constitution. Those in the minority on issues and votes were often considered to be morally in the wrong. It was this flawed structure that allowed injustices—such as slavery and the Mexican-American War—to take place. This system, Thoreau observed, was vulnerable to legislators and citizens who were often more concerned with commerce and territory than liberty.

The Utilitarian Political Structure

Like other social theorists such as Rousseau, Thoreau was interested in the unique relationship between individuals and their government. The utilitarian nature of the American government required citizens to acquiesce their individual wills with the understanding that the government would act in the interest of all, a situation Thoreau equated with living in hell.[69] Even if the individual did dissent, the government eventually imposed its will anyway. This ultimate allegiance subverted the fundamental aspect of humanity: the individual conscience. If this expedient and utilitarian structure of the American political system put the power of many in the hands of the few, it also assumed that the "majority rules" approach to policy decisions would ensure that the most morally correct decisions would be made. However, the voice of the majority was often determined through voting, which Thoreau viewed as an activity of chance where the individual conscience was counted only when it was in the majority. The act of voting did not adequately demonstrate individuals' abilities or willingness to physically act on what they saw as the morally correct decision. To Thoreau, voting was merely an effort to make one's desires known, not acting fervently on those desires. While voting did make governance more expedient, Thoreau believed it left the individual will and morality to chance:

> All voting is a sort of gaming, like checkers or backgammon, with a slight moral tinge to it, a playing with right and wrong, with moral questions; and

betting naturally accompanies it. The character of the voters is not staked. I cast my vote, perchance, as I think right; but I am not vitally concerned that that right should prevail. I am willing to leave it to the majority. Its obligation, therefore, never exceeds that of expediency. Even voting *for the right* is *doing* nothing for it. It is only expressing to men feebly your desire that it should prevail. A wise man will not leave the right to the mercy of chance, nor wish it to prevail through the power of the majority.[70]

Merely casting a vote in a ballot box once a year, Thoreau argued, mattered much less than the type of individual that person was on a daily basis.[71] Indeed, the fact that each person had a conscience suggested to Thoreau that decisions of right and wrong should be made by the individual conscience, not the majority. Because government had no conscience, Thoreau believed that the only obligation an individual really had was to do what he or she thought was morally correct, not what the government stated was right. He reasoned that if individuals were encouraged and allowed to use their individual consciences—to be individuals first and citizens second—the collective action of these individual consciences might affect an entire corporation or institution.

Law as Morality
Though the public often saw the two as analogous, Thoreau argued that law and policy should not be equated with morality.[72] The law, and the Constitution in particular, became the absolute standard by which expedient decisions were made. Thoreau speaks harshly of this "undue respect" for the law in his essay "Civil Disobedience," where he states that, more than respect for the law, society needed a respect for the right. Law itself did nothing to make humans more just. In fact, Thoreau believed that unconditional allegiance to the law often had the opposite effect of denigrating humans. Unconditional respect for law made humans into objects, or mere shadows of humanity who were living in body, but dead in intellect and conscience:

> It is not desirable to cultivate a respect for the law, so much as for the right. The only obligation which I have a right to assume is to do at any time what I think right. It is truly enough to say that a corporation has no conscience; but a corporation of conscientious men is a corporation *with* a conscience. Law never made men a whit more just; and, by means of their respect for it, even the well-disposed are daily made the agents of injustice. A common and natural result of an undue respect for law is, that you may see a file of soldiers, colonel, captain, corporal, privates, powder-monkeys, and all, marching in admirable order over hill and dale to the wars, against their wills, ay, against their

common sense and consciences, which makes it very steep marching indeed, and produces a palpitation of the heart. . . . Now, what are they? Men at all? Or small movable forts and magazines, at the service of some scrupulous man in power?[73]

When forced by the government, individuals would act against their own common sense and consciences, which transformed them from humans into malleable beings and movable machines at the service of those in power. This faithful adherence to the law frequently allowed widespread injustice to take place, with little outcry from the majority.

Subduing Dissent

If reverence to the law made a mockery of the individual conscience, refusing it came with steep costs. In a perverted twist, those who held steadfastly to the law and served it willingly, even when it was unjust, were regarded as good citizens, while those who rejected unjust law and served the nation by acting on their consciences were often considered enemies.[74] In Thoreau's view, martyrs and reformers such as John Brown, who served humanity and their nation by resisting the injustices of the government, were not simply treated as enemies of the state: they often paid the ultimate price. "Enemies" of the state were not confronted on moral or intellectual terms, but with the force of an American government that often used threats and its physical strength to impose its will. Thoreau saw this as a form of enslavement, since the mere threat of force could subdue people into serving or complying with the state's interest: "Thus the State never intentionally confronts a man's sense, intellectual or moral, but only his body, his senses. It is not armed with superior wit or honesty, but with superior physical strength."[75] The power and dominance of the majority, according to Thoreau, was not because the majority was right, or the most fair, but simply the strongest:

> After all, the practical reason why, when the power is once in the hands of the people, a majority are permitted, and for a long period continue, to rule, is not because they are most likely to be in the right, nor because this seems fairest to the minority, but because they are physically the strongest. But a government in which the majority rule in all cases cannot be based on justice, even as far as men understand it. Can there not be a government in which majorities do not virtually decide right and wrong, but conscience?—in which majorities decide only those questions to which the rule of expediency is applicable? Must the citizen ever for a moment, or in the least degree, resign his conscience to the legislator? Why has every man a conscience, then? I think that we should be men first, and subjects afterward.[76]

In government, might made right. This ability to employ physical force on the individual not only led to the manufacturing of "faithful citizens," it also resulted in additional government abuse of power in the form of slavery and war, which Thoreau saw as the ultimate sin against the individual and liberty.

The Power of Political Elites

Thoreau also recognized the role of political elites and the manner in which they used their power within the American government to protect the interests of certain groups at the expense of others. Authority figures, including judges, governors, and congressman, not only failed to protect the individual in society, they formulated policy in a manner that would subdue the individual citizen if it meant gains would be made for those in power. Thoreau was particularly critical of the government's unabashed promotion of the Mexican-American War (1846–1848) and slavery; he viewed the war and slavery as equivalent in their transgressions against humanity and the individual. Both of these injustices exemplified the government's interest in enacting the corrupt laws created by a small group of elites, rather than enforcing the laws of humanity. In the case of the Mexican-American War, military forces were used on a broad level to further the political and economic agendas of the elite, including slaveholders:

> The government itself, which is only the mode which the people have chosen to execute their will, is equally liable to be abused and perverted before the people can act through it. Witness the present Mexican war, the work of comparatively few individuals using the standing government as their tool; for, in the outset, the people would not have consented to this measure.[77]

The objectives and effects of the Mexican-American War represented social values that were antithetical to Thoreau's ideal of simplification: The war increased the numbers of American slaves, it drove many indigenous people from their land, and it brought more land to be exploited for the production of commodities. Indeed, Thoreau believed that the government's promotion of the war only helped fuel American's sense of entitlement. This entitlement was bound neither by national border—which had expanded into the Mexican territories of Texas, California, and New Mexico—nor by ethics. In "Slavery in Massachusetts," for example, he protests the enactment of the Fugitive Slave Law of 1850, which was passed by Congress to help slaveholders retrieve runaway slaves. The statute did not allow slaves the right to a jury trial or the opportunity to testify in their own defense. The federal leaders of the United States, he argues in "Slavery in Massachusetts," chose to use their influence and authority on behalf of the slaveholder rather than the slave, for the guilty rather than the innocent, and for injustice rather than justice.[78] This abuse of power in service of the interests of a limited group, rather than the individual citizen, outraged Thoreau:

> The whole military force of the State is at the service of a Mr. Suttle, a slaveholder from Virginia, to enable him to catch a man whom he calls his property; but not a soldier is offered to save a citizen of Massachusetts from being kidnapped! Is this what all these soldiers, all this *training*, have been for these seventy-nine years past? Have they been trained merely to rob Mexico and carry back fugitive slaves to their masters?[79]

Though he was outspoken against the war and slavery, Thoreau knew that because these leaders drew their livelihood and status from the current political system, they were unlikely to do anything to change it. To use C. Wright Mills's words, these figures were unable to think themselves away from their social situation and look at it anew, with an unbiased perspective.[80] Thoreau recognized the incapability of government leaders to adopt this view and to examine the realities of the very institution in which they worked. None was willing to resign from his authority position, even when his beliefs contradicted with the law. Nor were they able to observe the political system objectively outside of their own individual relation to it:

> I know that most men think differently from myself; but those whose lives are by profession devoted to the study of these or kindred subjects, content me as little as any. Statesmen and legislators, standing so completely within the institution, never distinctly and nakedly behold it. They speak of moving society, but have no resting-place without it. . . . Still, his quality is not wisdom, but prudence. The lawyer's truth is not truth, but consistency or a consistent expediency. . . . [H]e is unable to take a fact out of its merely political relations, and behold it as it lies absolutely to be disposed of by the intellect—what, for instance, it behooves a man to do here in America to-day with regard to slavery, but ventures, or is driven, to make some such desperate answer as the following, while professing to speak absolutely, and as a private man—from which what new and singular code of social duties might be inferred?[81]

> I am sorry to say that I doubt if there is a judge in Massachusetts who is prepared to resign his office, and get his living innocently, whenever it is required of him to pass sentence under a law which is merely contrary to the law of God. I am compelled to see that they put themselves, or rather are by character, in this respect, exactly on a level with the marine who discharges his musket in any direction he is ordered to. They are just as much tools, and as little men.

> Certainly, they are not the more to be respected, because their master enslaves their understandings and consciences, instead of their bodies.[82]

These "little men," as Thoreau referred to them, were unable to divorce their own personal interests and biography from their political decision making. Like the soldier who enslaved his body to the government by blindly following into an unjust war, political leaders enslaved their consciences to the state. Thoreau believed that the administration of justice by such authorities would be accidental, and that it would be better to trust the opinion of the masses than that of one government leader. However, Thoreau was not just suspicious of their decision making. He also questioned the ways by which these few authority figures were selected. In "Civil Disobedience" he argues that the choices were limited and certainly not representative of the population at large. The conventions held for the selections, he points out, were made of people who were politicians by profession, and editors, and others who had been bought. There were few independent men in the process who had a bone in their back "which you cannot pass your hand through."[83] Given the vested interests that elites had in the political system, the chance of social change coming from within the system itself was unlikely.

The Public Conscience
In Thoreau's view, the American political system helped perpetuate a public character that was marred with complacency in the face of injustice. While Thoreau did see the government as a forceful social structure that trampled on individual freedom, he also believed the American people did nothing to change their situation. He criticized all citizens, particularly his fellow New Englanders, who were more interested in commerce and the welfare of western territories than liberty and the injustice that was occurring in their own states.[84] While some fellow citizens were jailed or hanged for "loving liberty" by attempting to rescue slaves, most New Englanders were more concerned with how their resources were being allocated by Congress.

> Practically speaking, the opponents to a reform in Massachusetts are not a hundred thousand politicians at the South, but a hundred thousand merchants and farmers here, who are more interested in commerce and agriculture than they are in humanity, and are not prepared to do justice to the slave and to Mexico, *cost what it may.*[85]

Thoreau pointed out that most citizens focused their attention on free trade and waited for others to tend to injustices. Though some were, in opinion, opposed to slavery and war, their inaction spoke loudly of their character.

Their actions of regret, mild petition, and even voting led to little change. Instead they "sat with their hands in their pockets" and fell asleep while reading about the advancing war.[86] Worse than the inaction and complacency of the American people was their willing financial support of the American government. Thoreau particularly disdained the public inconsistency and hypocrisy on the Mexican-American War: Even as some citizens verbally denounced the war or even refused to serve, they offered a "substitute service" by sustaining and supporting the military action through their tax payments to the government. He saw this financial allegiance as proxy support of the government and its activities.[87]

Thoreau believed that the American citizenry's cooperation with and support for the government and its inactivity in the face of justice resulted from fear. Many citizens saw the government as a form of protection, and feared losing their property or being harassed if they did not continue their support:

> When I converse with the freest of my neighbors, I perceive that, whatever they may say about the magnitude and seriousness of the question, and their regard for the public tranquility, the long and the short of the matter is, that they cannot spare the protection of the existing government, and they dread the consequences to their property and families of disobedience to it. For my own part, I should not like to think that I ever rely on the protection of the State. But, if I deny the authority of the State when it presents its tax-bill, it will soon take and waste all my property, and so harass me and my children without end. This is hard. This makes it impossible for a man to live honestly, and at the same time comfortably in outward respects.[88]

Most citizens were not willing to sacrifice their comfort, and instead lived in fear of the consequences of noncompliance with government laws. Indeed, citizens' fear of their own government was evidence to Thoreau that individual liberty was not a reality. American freedom was an illusion—behind the ideals of liberty, democracy, and individuality lurked a blind respect for the law, a corrupt government, and a complacent citizenry that cared more about their pockets than their principles. To Thoreau, this political climate was anything but progress.

Though many take Thoreau's statement "The government is best which governs least"[89] as a call for no government, that interpretation is a misreading of his work. Thoreau was not calling for an end to government as an institution—he was not a "no-government man."[90] In fact, he writes in "Civil Disobedience" that he is searching for a better, more respectable government:

But, to speak practically and as a citizen, unlike those who call themselves no-government men, I ask for, not at once no government, but *at once* a better government. Let every man make known what kind of government would command his respect, and that will be one step toward obtaining it.[91]

Rather than a call for complete anarchy, Thoreau's work was an invocation to all citizens to determine for themselves what a respectable government would be and how the American political system was failing. To him, the government that trampled on the individual was certainly not the pinnacle of political evolution; nor was it the most effective, as many American citizens believed the U.S. government to be. Further progress could be made over the current system, which, in Thoreau's view, failed in its primary role to citizens: protecting the individual.

Indeed, while the rest of the world saw America as an experiment in political and economic progress, Thoreau looked beyond the surface to explore the effects of these new social structures on the attitudes and actions of the American individual. The relentless materialism, immoral government, and complacent citizenry created obstacles to individuality and human development. These obstacles were not only unnatural, they were built into the structure of the evolving American economic and political systems. Thoreau argued that they could and should be altered. However, many Americans saw western expansion and the evolving economic and political systems as signs of "progress" and American exceptionalism. Thoreau spent much of his writing scrutinizing this widely held belief. He deconstructed American ideals of "progress," examined the necessities of life, and even made efforts to explore what Americans might learn from more "savage" cultures, including American Indians. We will examine his exploration of these concepts in chapter 4.

Notes

1. Henry David Thoreau, "Walden," in *The Portable Thoreau*, rev. ed., ed. Carl Bode (New York: Penguin, 1987), 263.
2. Thoreau, "Walden," 292.
3. Henry David Thoreau, "Life without Principle," in *The Portable Thoreau*, rev. ed., ed. Carl Bode (New York: Penguin, 1987), 634.
4. Thoreau, "Life without Principle," 632, 637.
5. Thoreau, "Life without Principle," 632.
6. Thoreau compared the capitalist work to a machine in "Walden," 261: "Most men, even in this comparatively free country, through mere ignorance and mistake, are so occupied with the factitious cares and superfluously coarse labors of life that its finer fruits cannot be plucked by them. Their fingers, from excessive toil, are too

clumsy and tremble too much for that. Actually, the laboring man has not leisure for a true integrity day by day; he cannot afford to sustain the manliest relations to men; his labor would be depreciated in the market. He has no time to be anything but a machine."

7. James Guthrie, *Above Time: Emerson's and Thoreau's Temporal Revolutions* (Columbia, Missouri: University of Missouri Press, 2001), 1.

8. Guthrie, *Above Time*, 137.

9. Thoreau, "Walden," 369–70.

10. Guthrie, *Above Time*, 4.

11. Guthrie, *Above Time*, 138.

12. Guthrie, *Above Time*, 137.

13. Guthrie, *Above Time*, 280.

14. "Clock" time and "event" time are concepts developed by social psychologist Robert Levine in *A Geography of Time* (New York: Basic Books, 1998) to explain the difference in way cultures experience time. In clock time cultures, time is a commodity and there is less focus in human interaction. Event time cultures function less by a formal clock and tend to put more value on human relationships.

15. Thoreau, "Walden," 394.

16. Guthrie, *Above Time*, 62–64.

17. Thoreau discusses his ideas on transcending conventional time in *A Week on the Concord and Merrimack Rivers*, ed. Carl Hovde, William Howarth, and Elizabeth Hall Witherell (Princeton, NJ: Princeton University Press, 1980), 141.

18. For specific examples see Thoreau, "Walden," 266–67, and "Life without Principle," 634.

19. For example, Thoreau makes the following observation in "Walden," 277: "It is an interesting question how far men would retain their relative rank if they were divested of their clothes. Could you, in such a case, tell surely of any company civilized men which belonged to the most respected class?"

20. Thoreau, "Walden," 276–77.

21. Like Marx, Thoreau observed the fetishism of commercial products. See "Walden," 279.

22. Thoreau recounts his discussion of the reification of the market and its authority in the "Economy" chapter of "Walden," 280.

23. Thoreau discusses changing tastes of the market in "Walden," 281: "The childish and savage tastes of men and women for new patterns keeps how many shaking and squinting through the kaleidoscopes that they may discover the particular figure which this generation requires today. The manufacturers have learned that this is merely whimsical. Of two patterns which differ only by a few threads more or less of a particular color, the one will be sold readily, the other lie on the shelf, though it frequently happens that after the lapse of a season the latter becomes the most fashionable."

24. For example, in "Life without Principle," 633, Thoreau argues, "If a man walk in the woods for the love of them half of each day, he is in danger of being regarded

as a loafer; but if he spends his whole day as a speculator, shearing off those woods and making earth bald before her time, he is esteemed as an industrious and enterprising citizen."

25. See Thoreau, "Life without Principle," 633. Thoreau also points out in "Life without Principle," 631: "Commonly, if men want anything of me, it is only to know how many acres I make of their land—since I am a surveyor—or, at most, what trivial new I have burdened myself with. They never go for my meat; they prefer the shell."

26. For example, Thoreau states in "Life without Principle, 632: "If a man was tossed out of a window as an infant, and so made a cripple for life, or scared out of his wits by Indians, it is regretted chiefly because he was thus incapacitated for—business."

27. For example, in "Walden," 321–22, Thoreau states: "Not long since I was present at the auction of a deacon's effects, for his life had not been ineffectual:—'The evil that men do lives after them.' As usual, a great proportion was trumpery which had begun to accumulate in his father's day. . . . And now, after lying half a century in his garret and other dust holes, these things were not burned; instead of a bonfire, or purifying destruction of them, there was an auction, or increasing of them. The neighbors eagerly collected to view them, bought them all, and carefully transported them to their garrets and dust holes, to lie there till their estates are settled, when they will start again. When man dies he kicks the dust."

28. Lawrence Buell, *The Environmental Imagination: Thoreau, Nature Writing and the Formation of American Culture* (Cambridge, MA: Belknap Press of Harvard University Press, 1995), 276.

29. Thoreau wrote about the destruction of nature by removal of trees, forest fire, and the traces left by humans, including the logging industry.

30. Thoreau, "Walden," 367–68.

31. James McGrath, "Ten Ways of Seeing Landscapes in *Walden* and Beyond," in *Thoreau's Sense of Place: Essays in American Environmental Writing*, ed. Richard Schneider (Iowa City: University of Iowa Press, 2000), 153.

32. Thoreau, "Walden," 435.

33. Thoreau expands on these ideas in "The Ponds," a chapter of "Walden," 448.

34. See Bernard Quetchenbach, "Sauntering into the Industrial Wilderness," in *Thoreau's Sense of Place: Essays in American Environmental Writing*, ed. Richard Schneider (Iowa City: University of Iowa Press, 2000), 171. An example of this can be found in Thoreau's *The Maine Woods*, ed. Joseph Moldenhauer (Princeton, NJ: Princeton University Press, 1972), 93, where he was "strangely affected" when he saw a ring-bolt drilled into a rock on a solitary lake, which had been left behind by the loggers.

35. See Thoreau, "Walden," 441.

36. See Thoreau, "Walden," 445.

37. See Thoreau, "Walden," 445.

38. Michael Gilmore, *American Romanticism and the Marketplace* (Chicago: University of Chicago Press, 1985), 37.

39. See Thoreau, "Walden," 535–36.

40. Thoreau, "Walden," 422.

41. Henry David Thoreau, "Walking," in *The Portable Thoreau*, rev. ed., ed. Carl Bode (New York: Penguin, 1987), 598.

42. Buell, "Thoreau and the Natural Environment," 173; and Richard Schneider, "Introduction," in *Thoreau's Sense of Place: Essays in American Environmental Writing* (Iowa City: University of Iowa Press, 2000), 6.

43. Thoreau, *The Maine Woods*, 42.

44. Thoreau, "Walden," 440–41.

45. See Thoreau, *The Maine Woods*, 4–5.

46. Thoreau, *The Maine Woods*, 41.

47. Thoreau, *Journal*, ed. Bradford Torrey and Francis Allen (Boston, Massachusetts: 1906), VIII: 220.

48. Thoreau, "Walden," 523.

49. Thoreau, "Walden," 479.

50. Thoreau, "Walden," 519.

51. Schneider, "Introduction," 7. See Schneider's *Thoreau's Sense of Place* and Buell's *The Environmental Imagination* for discussion of "green" Thoreau.

52. Thoreau discusses the issue of public lands in *The Maine Woods*, 156; and Henry David Thoreau, *Wild Fruits: Thoreau's Rediscovered Last Manuscript*, ed. Bradley Dean (New York: W. W. Norton, 2000), 238.

53. Thoreau, "Walking," 602.

54. Tom Lynch, "The 'Domestic Air' of Wilderness: Henry Thoreau and Joe Polis in the Maine Woods," *Weber Studies* 14, no. 3 (Fall 1997).

55. Thoreau, *The Maine Woods*, 119.

56. Thoreau, "Walking," 602.

57. David James Duncan, "Foreword," in *Thoreau on Water: Reflecting Heaven*, ed. Robert Lawrence France (Boston: Mariner, 2001), xi.

58. For examples of Thoreau's exploration of the medicinal qualities of nature, see "Walking," 609–13, and *Wild Fruits*, 238.

59. See "Walking," 608, 627.

60. Gilmore, *American Romanticism*, 39.

61. Thoreau, "Walden," 261.

62. Thoreau, "Walden," 264.

63. See John Diggins, "Thoreau, Marx and the Riddle of Alienation," *Social Research* 39, no. 4 (1972): 571–98.

64. Diggins, "Thoreau, Marx and the Riddle of Alienation," 590, 598.

65. Diggins, "Thoreau, Marx and the Riddle of Alienation," 583.

66. Diggins, "Thoreau, Marx and the Riddle of Alienation," 584.

67. Diggins, "Thoreau, Marx and the Riddle of Alienation," 596.

68. Diggins, "Thoreau, Marx and the Riddle of Alienation," 594.

69. Thoreau speaks of this ultimate sin against the individual in "Slavery in Massachusetts," in *Reform Papers: The Writings of Henry D. Thoreau*, ed. Wendell Glick (Princeton, NJ: Princeton University Press, 1973), 106–7.

70. Thoreau, "Civil Disobedience," in *The Portable Thoreau*, rev. ed., ed. Carl Bode (New York: Penguin, 1987), 115–16.

71. Aside from "Civil Disobedience," Thoreau also discussed voting in "Slavery in Massachusetts," 103–104.

72. See "Slavery in Massachusetts," 103–4.

73. Thoreau, "Civil Disobedience," 111–12.

74. Government regulation of dissent and the ways in which is rewarded docile citizens is a major topic of Thoreau's "Civil Disobedience." See page 112, for example.

75. Thoreau, "Civil Disobedience," 126–27.

76. Thoreau, "Civil Disobedience," 111.

77. Thoreau, "Civil Disobedience," 109–10.

78. See Thoreau, "Slavery in Massachusetts," 94–95.

79. Thoreau, "Slavery in Massachusetts," 94–95.

80. C. Wright Mills, "The Promise," in *The Sociological Imagination* (New York: Oxford University Press, 1959), 3–24.

81. Thoreau, "Civil Disobedience," 133–35.

82. Thoreau, "Slavery in Massachusetts," 102–3.

83. Thoreau, "Civil Disobedience," 116.

84. For example, in "Slavery in Massachusetts," 102, Thoreau speaks vehemently against his fellow citizens' blind faith in the government, as in the following passage: "but while their brothers and sister are being scourged and hung for loving liberty, while—I might here insert all that slaver implies and is—it is the mismanagement of wood and iron that concerns them. Do what you will, O Government, with my wife and my children . . . I will obey your commands to the letter. It will indeed grieve me if you hurt them . . . but, nevertheless, I will pursue my chosen calling on this fair earth . . . Such is the attitude, such are the words of Massachusetts."

85. Thoreau, "Civil Disobedience," 114–15.

86. For example, in "Civil Disobedience," 115, Thoreau continues to criticize American complacency in the face of injustice: "There are thousands who are *in opinion* opposed to slavery and to the war, who yet in effect do nothing to put an end to them; . . . who even postpone the question of freedom to the question of free-trade, and quietly read the prices-current along with the latest advices from Mexico, and after dinner, and, it may be, fall asleep over them both. . . . They hesitate, and they regret, and sometimes they petition; but they do nothing in earnest and with effect. They will wait, well disposed, for others to remedy the evil, that they may no longer have to regret it."

87. In "Civil Disobedience," 117–18, Thoreau states: "See what gross inconsistency is tolerated. I have heard some of my townsmen say, 'I should like to have them order me out to help put down an insurrection of the slaves, or to march to Mexico—see if I would go'; and yet these very men have each, directly by their allegiance, and so indirectly, at least, by their money, furnished a substitute. The soldier is applauded who refuses to serve in an unjust war by those who do not refuse to sustain the unjust government which makes the war; is applauded by those whose own act and authority he

disregards and sets at naught; . . . Thus, under the name of Order and Civil Government, we are all made at last to pay homage to and support our own meanness."

88. Thoreau, "Civil Disobedience," 124.

89. Thoreau, "Civil Disobedience," 109.

90. Robert Richardson Jr., *Henry Thoreau: A Life of the Mind* (Berkeley and Los Angeles: University of California Press, 1986), 178; Lawrence Rosenwald, "The Theory, Practice and Influence of Thoreau's Civil Disobedience," in *A Historical Guide to Henry David Thoreau*, ed. William Cain (New York: Oxford University Press, 2000), 159.

91. Thoreau, "Civil Disobedience," 111.

CHAPTER FOUR

~

"Progress," Social Development, and Social Change

Perhaps Thoreau's greatest legacy lies in his ability to engage readers in self-examination by contrasting social definitions of progress and luxury with what we actually need to live a content life. Certainly, few Americans thinkers are as well known for their examination of "progress" than Thoreau. His most well known mantra "simplify, simplify" succinctly embodies his call to the individual to turn away from some of the more commonly held ideas of progress, such as the ability to afford expensive personal items. Indeed, for decades readers of *Walden* have been drawn to the idea of bare-bones living in a one-room cabin in the woods, a far cry from the sprawling homes we now construct in suburbs across America. These ideas have challenged readers to not only reexamine their own definitions of progress, but also to ask what the necessities of life really are. This legacy demonstrates that Thoreau's skepticism was not limited to social structures, such as the economy or the government; he was deeply concerned with "progress" and "social change," and in the illusions behind the ways in which society constructed such concepts. As a poet Thoreau set out to discover the true basics of daily living, and as a writer he aimed to reveal many of the superfluities of modern American life to his readers.

Within this chapter I examine Thoreau's analysis of progress by exploring his skepticism of broader society's perceptions of social advance in several spheres. The discussion will include his challenges to the ethnocentric and binary categories of development and progress, such as "civilized" and "savage" or "wealth" and "poverty," as well as his ideas on technological advances, science, and the possibilities of social reform.

Deconstructing Dichotomies of Progress

As a student of science in the nineteenth century, Thoreau had been working on his own theories of evolution, even before his in-depth reading of Darwin's *Origin of Species*.[1] Despite his interest in the science behind biological evolution, though, Thoreau was not a *social* evolutionist. Unlike figures such as Auguste Comte and Herbert Spencer, Thoreau did not believe that cultures progressed through particular stages in a linear fashion. To Thoreau, social change was neither unilateral nor categorically positive. Instead, he argued that modern civilization had, in many ways, regressed. While many Americans saw the broader changes in their country—technological advancement, increased accumulation of goods, and the emergence of science—as evidence of social progress, Thoreau questioned these measures by exploring the illusions behind such advances. He believed that progress was defined narrowly by America, with too much emphasis on outward luxury and technology. These advances, he believed, often created obstacles to real social progress, and brought little to Americans in terms of human development and equality.

The Civilized and the Savage

Thoreau was not convinced that modern America offered much, in terms of progress, over societies of the past. Like a number of sociologists, such as Jean-Jacques Rousseau and Emile Durkheim, he looked to the primitive life as a way to deconstruct common ideas about the "civilized" and the "savage." Through his readings, his studies of American Indians, and his own experiment at Walden Pond, Thoreau was seeking the primitive mind, not only to find out where society had made a turn for the worse, but also to examine the lessons earlier societies might provide to modern civilization.[2] His comparisons of the "civilized" and "savage" in *Walden*, in terms of housing, equality, and outward luxuries, help us frame Thoreau's ideas about where modern society stood in history and where it might progress from its current status. He used these comparisons to mount a critique of modern life, and, perhaps more importantly, to encourage his readers to develop their own broader measures and definitions of "progress," "civilization," and even "poverty." Ultimately, he wanted to determine what sacrifices, or regressions, the modern world had made because of its "progress," and what lessons the so-called civilized might learn from the "savage," so as to combine the best components of both worlds:

> He [the civilized] must have spent half of his life before his wigwam will be earned. Nevertheless, this points to an important distinction between the civ-

ilized man and the savage; and, no doubt, they have designs on us for our benefit, in making the life of a civilized people an institution, in which the life of an individual is to a great extent absorbed, in order to preserve and perfect that of the race. But I wish to show at what a sacrifice this advantage is at present obtained, and to suggest that we may possibly so live as to secure all the advantage without suffering any of the disadvantage.[3]

Though it was not the first time he addressed the issue of progress, Thoreau's most candid opposition to the strict boundaries that society had constructed in defining the "savage" and the "civilized" can be found in "Economy," the first chapter of *Walden*. It was here that he attempted to determine the "necessities of life," those facets of human life that are so important that few societies have done without them:

> By the words, *necessary of life*, I mean whatever, of all that man obtains by his own exertions, has been from the first, or from long use has become, so important to human life that few, if any, whether from savageness, or poverty, or philosophy, ever attempt to do without it. . . . The necessaries of life for man in this climate may, accurately enough, be distributed under the several heads of Food, Shelter, Clothing, and Fuel; for not till we have secured these are we prepared to entertain the true problems of life with freedom and prospect of successes.[4]

Thoreau explores several of these life necessities in this chapter. He specifically focuses on clothing and shelter by questioning what progress moderns had made in terms of these "necessities." In his discussion of shelter, for example, he compares the dwellings of the "savage" to those of the "civilized," and argues that modernity has provided better dwellings but not cheaper housing.[5] He also points out that the dwellings of the American Indian were just as warm as the best of English houses, and that the wigwam was quickly constructed and deconstructed. Not only were the American Indian dwellings more convenient, but in the "savage state" every family owned a home as "good as the best."[6] However, only half of the modern civilized owned a home. Worse, in the larger cities—considered the pinnacle of civilization—even less of the population owned their own place of dwelling. Thoreau believed that the savage owned a home because it cost so little and the civilized did not own because housing became expensive. He goes on in the same chapter to argue that if civilization is to be considered a "real advance" in the condition of humans, it must be demonstrated that it has produced better dwellings without rendering them more expensive. For Thoreau, housing was just one example of the many improvements of modern society that were aesthetic only. These advances came with costs, both economically and socially.

With such a narrow definition of progress, citizens were blind to the new problems that emerged with the advances of a capitalist society, including greater social stratification. Civilization, Thoreau believed, did not perpetuate the equality that existed in the primitive state. Even with all of the progress of modern life, Thoreau found the living conditions of some to be below that of the "savage." Though wealth abounded, many still lived in "poverty." He pointed to the class of people whose labor had allowed for "progress" to occur, specifically citing conditions in America, Ireland, and England.

> But how do the poor minority fare? Perhaps it will be found, that just in proportion as some have been placed in outward circumstances above the savage, others have been degraded below him. The luxury of one class is counterbalanced by the indigence of another. On the one side is the palace, on the other are the almshouse and "silent poor." . . . The mason who finishes the cornice of the palace returns at night perchance to a hut not so good as a wigwam. It is a mistake to suppose that, in a country where the usual evidences of civilization exist, the condition of a very large body of the inhabitants may not be as degraded as that of savages. . . . To know this I should not need to look farther than to the shanties which everywhere border our railroads, that last improvement in civilization; where I see in my daily walks human beings living in sties, and all winter with an open door, for the sake of light, without any visible, often imaginable, wood-pile, and the forms of both old and young are permanently contracted by the long habit of shrinking from cold and misery, and the development of all their limbs and faculties is checked. It certainly is fair to look at that class by whose labor the works which distinguish this generation are accomplished. Such too, to a greater or less extent, is the condition of the operatives of every denomination in England, which is the great workhouse of the world. Or I could refer you to Ireland, which is marked as one of the white or enlightened spots on the map. Contrast the physical condition of the Irish with that of the North American Indian, or the South Sea Islander, or any other savage race before it was degraded by contact with the civilized man. Yet I have no doubt that that people's rulers are as wise as the average of civilized rulers. Their condition only proves what squalidness may consist with civilization. I hardly need refer now to the laborers in our Southern States who produce the staple exports of this country, and are themselves a staple production of the South. But to confine myself to those who are said to be in *moderate* circumstances.[7]

Thoreau believed that it was necessary to explore the class differences that emerged as a result of economic progress, especially because those who had improved their standard of living often did so by standing on the shoulders of others, whether through slavery or paying low wages. The day laborers who constructed the "palaces" for the wealthy, he argued, eventually had to return to their "wigwams." The status of the "silent poor" had been degraded even below that of the savage. In the passage above Thoreau contrasted the railroad, a national sign of progress, with the poverty of the shanties that bordered the railroad. He also compared the conditions of the North American Indian to that of some Irish laborers, suggesting that the American Indian was actually better off, especially prior to contact with the civilized, which actually degraded the "savage race." To this end, Thoreau aimed to demonstrate to the reader that "squalidness" could, and did, exist within civilization, even in the most enlightened areas of Europe and the United States.

Redefining "Wealth" and "Poverty"

To Thoreau, there was nothing more "squalid" or repulsive than the American idea that "progress" and "civilization" could be measured by a citizen's possessions. Beyond pointing out that wealth and luxury were *not* life necessities, he forcefully argued that the American search for the comforts of life through consumption was actually a "positive hindrance to the elevation of mankind."[8] Yet, as he writes in *Walden* and "Life without Principle," Americans incorrectly believed that quality of life could be equated with standard of living:

> Most men, even in this comparatively free country, through mere ignorance and mistake, are so occupied with the factitious cares and superfluous coarse labors of life that its finer fruits cannot be plucked by them. Their fingers, from excessive toil, are too clumsy and tremble too much for that. Actually, the laboring man has not much leisure for a true integrity day by day; he cannot afford to sustain the manliest relations to men; his labor would be depreciated in the market. He has no time to be anything but a machine.[9]

> [T]here are those who style themselves statesmen and philosophers who are so blind as to think that progress and civilization depend on precisely this kind of [economic] interchange and activity—the activity of flies about a molasses-hogshead.[10]

To Thoreau, one of the "illusions" of these "modern improvements" was that they perpetually bred discontent.[11] He observed that his contemporaries were not content with the outward progress they had already made; their appetite for consumption continued to swell as they constructed additional artificial "needs," such as larger and more ornate homes.[12] In this downward spiral of sickness, desperation, and anxiety, individuals cheated themselves out of self-cultivation and their true potential. Such preoccupations with status and greed did not make the individual more civilized, but just the opposite: The individual was transformed into something less than human. Thoreau makes this parallel in *Walden* when he discusses the use of animals in farm labor:

> I am wont to think that men are not so much the keepers of herds as herds are the keepers of men, the former are so much the freer. Men and oxen exchange work; but if we consider necessary work only, the oxen will be seen to have greatly the advantage, their farm is so much the larger. . . . When men begin to do . . . but luxurious and idle work, with their assistance [animals], it is inevitable that a few do all the exchange work with the oxen, or, in other words, become the slaves of the strongest. Man thus not only works for the animal within him, but, for a symbol of this, he works for the animal without him.[13]

To Thoreau, this state of affairs signified anything but progressive social evolution. In works such as *Walden* and "Life without Principle," he challenges readers to reexamine their own definitions of wealth and poverty, and to consider alternative definitions to those put forth by popular culture, which are strictly tied to economic indicators. By arguing that "we are all poor in respect to a thousand savage comforts, thought surrounded by luxuries,"[14] he encourages us to question the meaning of "poverty." Equally important, he argued that other forms of poverty rampant in American life—such as a lack of individual freedom, or the neglect of intellectual, emotional, or spiritual development—certainly were a greater affront to the individual than material poverty. Though Americans were surrounded by luxury, Thoreau believed it mired them in an abject poverty of the soul. By fixating on accumulating the best and newest, they enjoyed "lives of quiet desperation"—a shallow reflection of what humanity was meant to be at its fullest.[15]

Learning from the Savage

Because civilization did bring some negatives, Thoreau believed it was important for individuals to be open to what could be learned from the past. He was interested in combining the best of both the "savage" and civilized worlds.[16] Contemporary Americans could learn a lot from the "savage" about simplicity, independence, and nature, and in the process, they could redefine modern ideas and definitions of "progress." Thoreau aimed to reverse many of the obstacles to individual liberty—in his own life and the lives of his readers—by shifting examination and celebration from the shallow wonders of modern society to the lessons of the past, which could be yoked to allow for greater self-cultivation and development. In *Walden* he points to his own experiment of adopting some of the ways of the "savage" to make his case: "I am convinced, that if all men were to live as simply as I then did, thieving and robbery would be unknown. These take place only in communities where some have got more than is sufficient while others have not enough."[17]

Thoreau was particularly impressed with the simplicity of the "savage." While the civilized human had become a "tool" to desires and work, primitive people, through living in simplicity, were able to be "sojourners in nature" and to engage in contemplation and self-development:

> The very simplicity and nakedness of man's life in the primitive ages imply this advantage, at least, that they left him still but a sojourner in nature. When he was refreshed with food and sleep, he contemplated his journey again. He dwelt, as it were, in a tent in this world, and was either threading the valleys, or crossing the plains, or climbing the mountain-tops. But lo! men have become the tools of their tools. The man who independently plucked the fruits when he was hungry is become a farmer; and he who stood under a tree for shelter, a housekeeper. We now no longer camp as for a night, but have settled down on earth and forgotten heaven.[18]

Thoreau suggests that civilized societies should imitate the tradition of nonaccumulation practiced by some "savage nations," where excess possessions were purged each year.[19] To him, these characteristics of the primitive lifestyle were more significant and worthwhile for the development of humans than the modern preoccupation with consuming the newest fashions. A more simplistic lifestyle, rather than an existence as a "tool" of work and material desires, would allow for the more important "business" of self-cultivation to take place. Convinced that internal progress was superior to external wealth, he looked to civilizations of the past, which had already demonstrated that quality of life did not depend on opulence or outward luxuries:

> With respect to luxuries and comforts, the wisest have ever lived a more simple and meagre life than the poor. The ancient philosophers, Chinese, Hindoo, Persian, and Greek, were a class than which none has been poorer in outward riches, none so rich inward. . . . What is the nature of the luxury that enervates and destroys nations? Are we sure that there is none of it in our own lives?[20]

Other civilizations had achieved greatness without indulgence and greed. Yet, to Thoreau, America had regressed by constructing a wholly different and unhealthy definition of progress that fixated on material achievements.

Thoreau also believed that the so-called primitives could offer lessons on the human benefits of the natural environment, which the "civilized" Americans were rapidly clearing and processing as a commodity to be sold in the marketplace. In "Walking" he argues that society is in danger when wilderness is destroyed: "In Wilderness is preservation of the world."[21] Since freedom was to be found in nature, not in a culture that trampled on individualism, nature had the ability to rejuvenate the world.[22] The "savage," by living in nature, had allowed this rejuvenation, but civilized society had forgotten this lesson. To demonstrate this Thoreau again looks to successful civilizations of the past to prove that American ideas of cultural progress and the value of nature were flawed:

> The civilized nations—Greece, Rome, England—have been sustained by the primitive forests which anciently rotted where they stand. They survive as long as the soil is not exhausted. Alas for human culture! Little is to be expected of a nation, when the vegetable mould is exhausted, and it is compelled to make manure of the bones of its fathers.[23]

There were lessons to be learned from these earlier civilizations, from the benefits of a more simplistic lifestyle and the ability to feel at home in nature, to an independence of mind that was sacrificed in modern life. To those who sought rejuvenation and comfort in consumer products while destroying nature in the process, Thoreau offered earlier, "less civilized," societies as a model for a new path to progress. Rather than blindly trudging toward individual and social destruction, true progress could begin by unlocking some of the lessons of the more "primitive" and by recognizing the value and strength to be found in those presumably "less civilized" societies.

Thoreau and Spencer

At the same time that Thoreau was questioning many of the commonly held American ideas of progress and social evolution, a British sociological theorist named Herbert Spencer was applying natural law and the scientific understanding of evolutionary theory to social life. Born just three years after Thoreau, Spencer spent his career advocating the idea of social Darwinism by arguing that the laws of evolution also applied to societies. From this perspective, even in human social life only the strong would survive. Spencer saw inequality and hunger not as social ills, but as ways that society eliminated its weaker members. His ideas about progress, social change, and sociology have played an important role in the historical development of sociological thought. As early as the 1860s, when Thoreau and Spencer were in their forties, Spencer's works were already popular and influential in America.[24]

At first glance, we could not find two more different social critics. Spencer's "survival of the fittest" approach to society seems to conflict with Thoreau's calls for dissent and social justice. Even more divergent are their views on the evolution of society and their individual definitions of social "progress." Ironically, though, Thoreau and Spencer do share some common ground. Both men were staunch individualists who believed that all social phenomena emerged from the foundation of the individual. For society to progress, they believed, the individual conscience must be free of restraints, especially from government. Spencer and Thoreau also shared the belief that government should occupy a minimal role in social life, and that its main function should be protection of individual liberty. Like Thoreau, Spencer wrote about the relationship between the individual and government in his essay entitled "The Man versus the State" (1884). In general, neither believed in collective action as a method of social reform. In fact, both men had a strong dislike for "do-gooders" and reformers. Because of their wide-ranging intellectual interests, their works are drawn on by a number of disciplines. Spencer and Thoreau employed the natural sciences and scientific methods in their efforts to understand the world. Though they arrived at different conclusions, both also used historical-comparative analysis to examine different stages of societies across different time periods. Thoreau's historical-comparative analysis resulted in his deconstruction of the concepts of "civilized and savage" as well as his extensive "Indian Notebooks." Spencer, on the other hand, used historical-comparative analysis to develop typologies of social stages and types of societies.

Despite some similarities, Thoreau's postmodern approach to development and progress is certainly at odds with Spencer's more linear and modernist view of social evolution. Spencer believed that primitive people were impulsive and selfish, lacking the self-control possessed by moderns, whom he believed were more integrated into collective life.[25] Though he did not take an absolute unilinear approach to the evolution of society, he did argue that societies typically progress from chaos to order. Spencer's measures of developmental progress included differentiation, complexity, mutual dependence, and increased social integration—all of which contradict basic Thoreauvian ideals of progress such as simplicity and self-reliance. Like Spencer, Thoreau understood and accepted evolutionary theory as a basic law of biological progression. He even conducted his own studies of plant life to explore the realities of evolution in nature. However, where Spencer was willing to apply some ideas of evolutionary theory to social life, Thoreau was not. His entire project of exploring American ideals of progress was an attempt to unveil the logic behind evolutionary assumptions about the inferiority of the "savage" and "primitive" and superiority of the "civilized," assumptions that Spencer promoted. Indeed, Spencer would have scoffed at Thoreau's arguments in *Walden* and "Walking" demonstrating that there were virtues and lessons to be learned from the more "primitive and savage lifestyle."

Spencer's organic view of society resulted in other ways in which his approach to society differed from Thoreau's. Like Thoreau, Spencer saw the individual as the basic building block of social life, but Spencer was also a realist—he believed that society was a separate entity from the individual.[26] Despite his staunch individualism, Spencer's organic view of society made it impossible for him to discount collective life.[27] And though he rejected utilitarianism in its strictest sense, Spencer was concerned with the function and utility of different institutions as society become more complex and differentiated. If society's parts were to work in equilibrium, like those of an organism, they had to function collectively.

Thoreau, on the other hand, would not concede that society was separate from the individual. He took a nominalist approach to society: it was nothing more than the sum of its parts, which were made up of individuals. The belief that society took on a life of its own, and was somehow outside of the control of the individuals that comprised, was flawed. While Thoreau spent his share of time analyzing social institutions such as the government and the economic system, he saw individuals as the atoms of these institutions, and, as such, he held the individual accountable for the structure and acts of these institutions he or she composed. To Thoreau, the functionality or dysfunctionality of the institution did not depend on its complexity, its utilitarian function as part of the greater "social organism of society," or the part it played in division of labor. Rather than Spencer's social utilitarian analysis of the functions performed by particular institutions, Thoreau's social analysis was an effort to determine the extent to which all social institutions served the same function: protecting and developing the individual.

Thoreau and Durkheim

Thoreau's efforts to analyze modern social development while keeping the individual primary are even more evident if his ideas are contrasted with the work of Emile Durkheim. Like Spencer before him, Durkheim believed that society exists on its own (sui generis) and that constraints external to the individual actually served a functional social purpose; the authority, moral guidance, and rituals provided by society made human social life more cohesive and integrated.[28] However, Durkheim lacked the concern for the individual that Thoreau, and even Spencer, possessed. Instead, Durkheim focused his analysis on the ways modernity dealt with the "problem" of controlling and integrating the individual conscience for the good of society. He even argued that it was the individual who *needed* society and its guiding mechanisms in order to become fully human, an idea that would have been flatly rejected by Thoreau and other Transcendentalists. From a Thoreauvian point of view, these were arguments that far undervalued the interior virtues of the individual and greatly overemphasized the positive aspects of social life. Whereas Durkheim sought to better understand social regulation as a functional component of society, Thoreau believed that the individual should seek to understand and unveil social forces so that they could be resisted; with a better understanding of the ways in which society tried to regulate daily life, the individual would be better armed for liberty.

If Durkheim and Thoreau had inverted intentions for analyzing society, their overall views of the tribulations and advantages of modernity were equally opposed. Durkheim was concerned with effects that modern development was having on the ability of traditional social mechanisms to generate social order and integration. One of the most troubling dilemmas of modern life, particularly with respect to social integration, was anomie—a state of normlessness in which the individual feels disconnected and alone. To Durkheim, anomie resulted from a decline in collective morality and an increase in individualism. But while anomie, declining morality, and individualism threatened social order and stability, Durkheim recognized that other by-products of modernity brought increased social integration. In one of his most well-known works, *The Division of Labor* (1893), Durkheim examines the ways in which the increased specialization of labor within industrial capitalism lent to social solidarity in modern society. Human reliance on economic division of labor, Durheim argued, produced greater human cooperation, bonding, and social solidarity.

Thoreau's views of modernity reverse the logic and moral reasoning used by Durkheim. While Durkheim believed that individual anomie and alienation resulted from a lack of social regulation, Thoreau saw a reverse cause: Alienation was the result of too much social regulation of the individual conscience and the loss of self-reliance that resulted from specialization of labor. Their divergent views of modernity stem, in part, from their moral approaches to society. Durkheim believed that the moral requirements of social life included sacrificing some individual desires and obeying social rules.[29] Thoreau, on the other hand, argued that the individual had a moral duty to his or her conscience to resist external social pressures. Durkheim saw natural law materializing in social life through division of labor, while Thoreau saw the reliance on others and the influence of society on the individual as a violation of human nature.

Technology and Science

While Thoreau championed the past as a model for the present, eighteenth-century Americans increasingly turned toward the future, as the railroad and other industrial innovations helped fuel the public's appetite for technology. As "developed" or "civilized" countries' obsession with technology has grown in the twenty-first century, some individuals have turned to Thoreau's work in their rejection of technological "necessities," such as the cell phone, e-mail, or Palm Pilot™. Many critics of modernity see Thoreau as a figure who was antitechnology—a "mensch" in a material world. In truth, he was a student of science, a land surveyor, and a pencil manufacturer who was intrigued with technology and measurement. Yet his interest did not preclude him from being skeptical of technological advance as an ultimate measure of progress. To Thoreau, technology could be a means of improving one's life, but to many Americans it had become a greater end or goal. Thoreau lamented that the resources put toward technological development had trumped those put toward personal development.

During Thoreau's lifetime the railroad system extended across the United States, the telegraph enabled coast-to-coast communication, and science began to emerge as a means of understanding the world. He was eager to point out that there were many illusions behind measuring progress by standards such as the distance of the railroad tracks. For example, luxury was often put above safety in the design of the trains, many citizens could still not afford the fare to ride, and the new mobility created by the train did little to end the poverty of those who laid the tracks.[30] Thoreau was also skeptical of new advances being made in communication technology. Progress, he believed, was not in the technology itself, but in the content it carried. In *Walden* he scoffs at the construction of a magnetic telegraph from Maine to Texas, questioning whether either side would have anything important to say; he also criticizes American newspapers for simply printing the gossip of the day. He even takes a cynical approach to the plans to tunnel under the Atlantic to bring the Old World and the New World closer together, and wonders if the most important news of the day would be that the princess "has the whooping cough."[31]

These words, written in the mid-1800s, demonstrate a keen insight into popular culture and also foretell the conundrum of modern media, where celebrity whereabouts are broadcast as "news alerts," and the sheer quantity of television channels does little to provide anything of value worth watching. While citizens of the modern era increasingly became slaves to their own technology, Thoreau believed it should have been the other way around—technology should serve the development of the individual. Similar to his view on the capitalist marketplace, this fetishism of technology was anything but progressive. Even though society had made advances in means of transportation and communication, true progress, he argued, should be measured by the content of the character being transported in the cross-continental train or the content of the information being sent across the country, not the technology itself.

Science, Inquiry, and the Boundaries of "Knowledge"

Beyond these new technologies, new methods of inquiry also caught Thoreau's eye. Laura Dassow Walls has written a comprehensive examination of Thoreau's knowledge and use of science, a topic that has not received broader attention because of the strict boundaries that have emerged between different fields of knowledge.[32] Walls reveals a different side of Thoreau than is familiar to those who know him only as a "literary figure." She points out that as a Transcendentalist Thoreau was interested in the metaphysical questions of how to bridge the gap between ignorance and knowledge, how we arrive at facts, and how facts become knowledge.[33] Coupled with his love of nature, it should be no surprise that Thoreau developed an interest in scientific inquiry. He studied botany, geology, zoology, entomology, ornithology, and meteorology, and he actively read the works of contemporary scientists such as Alexander von Humboldt and Darwin.[34] Thoreau was also acutely aware of Americans' fascination with measurement and categorization, including statistics, and was himself a measurer by trade.[35] Aside from his duties as a land surveyor, Thoreau spent ten years compiling data and charts on birds, leaves, and fish to create a conceptual model of the archetypal year.[36] He became an active member of the scientific community, collected specimens for Louis Agassiz (a prominent scientist at Harvard) and was elected to the Boston Society of Natural History.[37] Three years before he died Thoreau was appointed to Harvard's Visiting Committee in Natural History.[38] The work he did on the succession of forest trees later in his life is now considered to be a ground-breaking work in technical ecology.[39]

Walls points out that just as he questioned the binary categories of "wealth and poverty" or "civilized and savage," Thoreau also attempted to mediate the dichotomy between literature and science, a schism that was not as wide in Thoreau's time as it is today.[40] Although Thoreau's actions and writings demonstrate that he appreciated science for its ingenuity, preciseness, and ability to chart nature, he struggled with science as the ultimate progression of knowing the world.[41] Even though he was engaging in scientific activities until the final year of his life, Thoreau's journal entries also attest to the fact that he became increasingly disenchanted with the possibilities of science. In his most critical and conflicted stances toward science, he argued that it limited human knowledge with its conventional categorization and its dry, often mechanical approach to natural phenomena. There was much more to be seen and experienced than modern science could provide, and it was certainly not, Thoreau argued, the ultimate progression of inquiry.

Instead, the scientist's view was unnaturally narrow. In particular, the language and categorization used by scientists structured observation in a way that Thoreau believed was restrictive. He recognized that the mere way in which humans talked about objects shaped how they viewed them, which led him to argue that scientific nomenclature often inhibited, rather than enhanced, the search for and communication of knowledge:[42]

> Our scientific names convey a very partial information only; they suggest certain thoughts only. It does not occur to me that there are other names for most of these objects, given by most people who stood between me and them, who had better senses than our race. How little I know of that arbor-vitae when I have learned only what science can tell me! It is but a word. It is not a tree of life. But there are twenty words for the tree and its different parts which the Indian gave, which are not in our botanies, which imply a more practical and vital science. . . . No science does more than arrange what knowledge we have of any class of objects. But, generally speaking, how much more conversant was the Indian with any wild animal or plant than we are, and in his language is implied all that intimacy, as much as ours is expressed in our language. . . . The Indian stood nearer to wild nature than we. . . . We have but the most distant knowledge of them [wildlife]. . . . It was a new light when my guide gave me Indian names for things which I had only scientific ones before. In proportion as I understood the language, I saw them from a new point of view.[43]

To Thoreau, a poet and writer, language implied how conversant humans were with nature.[44] He pointed out that other societies, including North American Indians, had a variety of words that suggested the vitality of natural phenomena, which allowed these groups to have a more intimate relationship with nature.[45] To the scientist, though, discovery was no more than the naming of an object. Scientific understanding did not extend beyond measuring, naming, and categorizing, which amounted to little progress. Thoreau even equated modern scientific descriptions to mathematical formulas that did nothing to report all the "sensations" experienced when confronting natural phenomena. Not only was this type of inquiry vacant of perception and interest, but its contributions became little more than numbers on a page or specimens in a bottle:

Modern botanical descriptions approach ever nearer to the dryness of an algebraic formula, as if x + y were = to a love letter. It is the keen joy and discrimination of the child who has just seen a flower for the first time and comes running in with it to its friends. How much better to describe your object in fresh English words rather than these conventional Latinisms! He has really seen, and smelt, and tasted, and reports his sensations.[46]

Though science may sometimes compare herself to a child picking up pebbles on the seashore, that is a rare mood with her; ordinarily her practical belief is that it is only a few pebbles which are not known, weighed and measured. A new species of fish signifies hardly more than a name. See what is contributed in the scientific reports. One counts the fin-rays, another measures the intestines, a third daguerreotypes a scale, etc., etc.; Otherwise there's nothing to be said. . . .

What is the amount of the discovery to me? It is not that I have got it in a bottle, that it has got a name in a book, but that I have a little fishy friend in a pond. How was it when the youth first discovered fishes? . . . Generally the boy loses some of his perception and his interest in the fish; he degenerates into a fisherman or an ichthyologist.[47]

Thoreau feared that over time the human perception of natural phenomena would degenerate, as science and conventional language imposed their categories and structure on the way humans thought about nature.[48] Taken alone, this objective view would omit human imagination from inquiry and alienate humanity from its subject matter by providing no more than a mechanical knowledge of life. This would result in a regression of the relationship between humans and nature. Science as a sole method of inquiry would diminish the subjective experience that Thoreau so valued as a Transcendentalist:

There is no such thing as pure *objective* observation. Your observation, to be interesting, *i.e.* to be significant, must be *subjective*. The sum of what the writer of whatever class has to report is simply some human experience, whether he be poet or philosopher or man of science. . . . If it is possible to conceive of an event outside to humanity, it is not of the slightest significance, though it were the explosion of a planet. . . . I look over the report of the doings of a scientific association and am surprised that there is so little life to be reported; I am put off with the dry technical terms.[49]

Scientific measures, specimen collections, categorizing, and naming, Thoreau believed, were insignificant without a larger understanding of nature's personal and moral value to humans; these mechanical understandings of nature that science provided did nothing to demonstrate its significance for human existence. Thoreau came to recognize that progress toward breaching the chasm between ignorance and knowledge would require a broader project than science alone could offer.[50]

This realization led Thoreau to attempt to move beyond conventional knowledge into "atmospheres unknown."[51] He wanted to see the world around him with an original view and forget all that was presumed when a strictly scientific approach was taken. He specifically sought a more balanced form of inquiry that was more subjective, alive, and significant than science. In order to get nearer to natural objects, Thoreau echoed a message strikingly similar to one of the first lessons of sociology, articulated by Peter Berger: that nothing is what you have taken it be.

> It is only when we forget all learning that we begin to know. I do not go nearer by a hair's breadth to any natural object so long as I presume that I have an introduction to it by some learned man. To conceive of it with a total apprehension I must for the thousandth time approach it as something totally strange. If you would make acquaintance with the ferns, you must forget your botany. You must get rid of what is commonly called *knowledge* of them. Not a single scientific term or distinction is the least to the purpose, for you would fain perceive something, and you must approach the subject totally unprejudiced. You must be aware that *no thing* is what you have taken it to be . . . you have got to be in a different state than the common.[52]

> As it is important to consider Nature from the point of view of science, remembering the nomenclature and system of men, and so, if possible, go a step further in that direction, so it is equally important often to ignore or forget all that men presume that they know, and take an original and unprejudiced view of Nature, letting her make what impressions she will on you, as the first men, and all children and natural men still do. For our science, so called, is always more barren and mixed up with errors than our sympathies are.[53]

To proceed in this different direction, it was necessary to look at things without the sterile categories that science imposed on natural phenomena. The observer needed to leave behind the "harness" that prior knowledge often created, and approach subject the matter as if was strange and novel.[54] Arguing that newer modern scientists had not made significant advances in their understanding of natural phenomena, Thoreau believed it was necessary to look to the past. As he stated in his journals, there were lessons to be learned from earlier naturalists:

The old naturalists were so sensitive and sympathetic to nature that they could be surprised by the ordinary events of life. It was an incessant miracle to them, and therefore gorgons and flying dragons were not incredible to them. The greatest and saddest defect is not credulity, but our habitual forgetfulness that our science is ignorance.[55]

Earlier writers, such as Pliny and Aristotle, had more wonder for the ordinary aspects of life and took pleasure in describing nature, while new scientists were more concerned with simple measurement and categorization.[56] As Thoreau struggled to define the "true scientist," and a more holistic way of seeing he world, he turned to figures and methods outside the fields of science. His search to bridge the gap between ignorance and knowledge eventually led him to combine the methods of the poet-philosopher with the scientist—to realize true progress of knowledge he turned to interdisciplinary inquiry.

In his own attempts to move beyond conventional knowledge into "atmospheres unknown," Thoreau sought to combine the eye of the artist, the linguistic capabilities and moral understanding of the poet-philosopher, and the preciseness of the scientist.[57] Walls points out that as Thoreau pursued a way of knowing that was more relational to humans, he believed that it would be the poet-philosopher who would transform science into a "con-science," or "moral knowledge," by combining nature, philosophy, and science.[58] Thoreau's attempts at this integration are evident through his journals and other writings—as a scientist he collected facts of nature, and as a philosopher he made deductions of facts and sought to establish theories.[59] He knew that this task of integration would not be easy:

[I]t requires different intentions of the eye and of the mind to attend to different departments of knowledge! How differently the poet and the naturalist look at objects! A man sees only what concerns him. A botanist absorbed in the pursuit of grasses does not distinguish the grandest pasture oaks. He as it were tramples down oaks unwittingly in his walk.[60]

It is impossible for the same person to see things from the poet's view and that of the man of science. I realize that men may be born to a condition of mind at which others arrive in middle age by the decay of their poetic faculties.[61]

Yet it was necessary to combine these two ways of seeing—the poet would provide the more subjective and conscious approach needed to create the "true scientist." In *Excursions* (1842) Thoreau defines this true scientist as one who possessed a deeper and finer experience, which included an "Indian wisdom."[62] Max Oelschlaeger, author of *The Idea of Wilderness* (1991) believes that Thoreau was drawn to this characteristic because it brought to inquiry all that the scientist lacked: a sense of sympathy, discovery, and significance to the understanding of nature.[63] It was the more qualitative and humanistic approach that Thoreau desired. Oelschlaeger also argues that Thoreau was attracted to Indian wisdom because it allowed him to approach phenomena differently than the scientist did by not imposing timeless names and categories; instead, this method sought a more pre-social meaning of natural objects by renewing knowledge of the primitive, the savage, Indian, and archaic relation with natural objects.[64]

It was this interdisciplinary approach of the poet-philosopher, Thoreau believed, that would advance science in a new direction of progress, into the "atmospheres unknown" he sought in his own inquiry. In Walls's words, Thoreau was a "theorist at the crossroads of disciplines" who engaged in original, "innovative and experimental modes of thinking and writing."[65] This approach certainly presents a challenge to the stringent modern disciplinary boundaries that have evolved between various fields of inquiry. Just as Thoreau has called on readers to redefine their own definitions of poverty or wealth, his ideas on inquiry call us to question what progress we have made in the twenty-first century by enforcing such strict boundaries around the methods by which we attempt to acquire knowledge. Thoreau's ideas about "progressing knowledge" and his critique of emerging American ideals of intellectual progress offer important lessons to academia in general, and sociology in particular. His approach to knowledge certainly provides a model for what a more interdisciplinary inquiry might look like in practice.

Social Change

In addition to his ideas on the illusions of progress and how it was defined in relation to economic, technological, and scientific development, Thoreau had clear ideas on how political progress could be attained, particularly in terms of the question of social change and social action. While Thoreau is well known for his influence on Gandhi and King's nonviolent cooperation movements, his writings do demonstrate the progression of his own ideas about creating social change. From some of his earlier works, such as "The Service" (1902), "Paradise (to be) Regained" (1843), and "Reform and Reformers" (1844), to later works such as "Resistance to Civil Government" (1849), "Slavery in Massachusetts" (1854), and "A Plea for Captain John Brown" (1859), Thoreau shifted from pacifist to activist-reformer and eventually to a willingness to use force in order to effect social change.[66] Early on, particularly in *Walden*, Thoreau was adamant about his dislike of reformers and philanthropic organizations.[67] He was highly skeptical of the intentions and moral characteristics of both groups:

> As for doing good, that is one of the professions that is full.[68]

> A man is not a good man to me because he will feed me if I should be starving, or warm me if I should be freezing, or pull me out of a ditch if I should ever fall into one. I can find you a Newfoundland dog that will do as much. Philanthropy is not love of man in the broadest sense.[69]

Works such as *Walden* and "Paradise (to be) Regained" demonstrate Thoreau's earlier belief that only individual self-reform, self-development, and self-cultivation would lead to a better society. His faith in self-reform as a catalyst for social change can be clearly seen in "Paradise (to be) Regained," which was a critique of J. A. Etzler's essay "The Paradise within Reach of all Men, without Labor, by Powers of Nature, and Machinery, An Address to all Intelligent Men" (1842). Etzlers's work suggested that within ten years of the article's publication, cutting-edge technology, such as new facilities for transportation, aerial locomotion, and the navigation of space, would provide for all human needs. Within his critique of Etzler's essay, we can see some of Thoreau's early ideas of reform:

> Alas! This is the crying sin of the age, this want of faith in the prevalence of a man. Nothing can be effected but by one man. He who wants help wants everything. True, this is the condition of our weakness, but it can never be the means of our recovery. We must first succeed alone, that we may enjoy our success together. . . . In this matter of reforming the world, we have little faith in corporations; not thus was it first formed.[70]

Here Thoreau professed his faith in the individual succeeding alone in reform, which he believed started with inner moral transformation.[71] While Etzler argued that the worldly changes would reform the individual, Thoreau believed he had the solution backward.[72]

As American society changed, though, so did Thoreau's ideas on progressive reform. When Texas petitioned for admission to the Union, the South stood to increase its influence on the national political scene.[73] With the acceptance of Texas into the Union in 1845, war with Mexico—which did not accept Texas's succession—began. Thoreau's shift in attitude about reform can be seen in his written response to the government activity during the time of the Mexican-American War, "Civil Disobedience." At this point, Thoreau realized that something more than self-reform was needed to change social evil, and his refusal to pay the poll tax was his demonstration that action from principle could be revolutionary, creating political progress.[74] Within "Civil Disobedience" Thoreau asks his readers why they should give in to oppressive government forces, which, he points out, are both brute and inhumane. Since these forces were not natural, they could be resisted and altered.[75] Arguing that the friction caused by the machine of government was organized oppression, Thoreau calls for a revolt, including breaking the law, if necessary. He argues that acting on individual principle, which he defines as the perception and performance of the right, would change things.[76] For the first time, he specifically uses the words "rebel" and "revolutionize":

> But when the friction comes to have its machine, and oppression and robbery are organized, I say, let us not have such a machine any longer. In other words, when a sixth of the population of a nation which has undertaken to be the refuge of liberty are slaves, and a whole country is unjustly overrun and conquered by a foreign army, and subjected to military law, I think that it is not too soon for honest men to rebel and revolutionize. What makes this duty the more urgent is the fact that the country so overrun is not our own, but ours is the invading army.[77]

These sentiments were a marked change from his previous approach to reform. Thoreau used "Civil Disobedience" to try to convince readers that they should take social injustice as seriously as they would take personal injustice. Rather than just inner moral transformation, Thoreau's own ideas of reform had progressed to the belief that *individual action from principle*, such as his refusal to pay the poll tax, was required to change social relations drastically.

Thoreau's view of progress through social action can also be found in the mood of "Slavery in Massachusetts," which represents a drastic shift from his earlier writings.[78] New demands, realizations, and rhetoric can be seen in this work, which was a response to the Fugitive Slave Law of September 1850. The law authorized the return of all slaves, including those who no longer lived in slave states. Thoreau was appalled at the use of military force to enforce this law, which protected the interests of some (slaveholders) and not others (slaves).[79] Recognizing this injustice, Thoreau came to the realization that he could not live peaceably in an environment where the individual was being trampled. Even his relaxation in nature was tainted by the current social situation. When freedom was threatened, self-cultivation was not possible:[80]

> I have lived for the last month . . . with the sense of having suffered a vast and indefinite loss. At last it occurred to me that what I had lost was a country. I had never respected the government near to which I lived, but I had foolishly thought that I might manage to live here, minding my private affairs, and forget

it. For my part, my old and worthiest pursuits have lost I cannot say how much of their attraction, and I feel that my investment in life here is worth many per cent less since Massachusetts last deliberately sent back an innocent man, Anthony Burns, to slavery. I dwelt before, perhaps, in the illusion that my life passed somewhere only *between* heaven and hell, but now I cannot persuade myself that I do not dwell *wholly within* hell. The site of that political organization called Massachusetts is to me morally covered with volcanic scoriae and cinders, such as Milton describes in the infernal regions. If there is any hell more unprincipled than our rulers, and we, the ruled, I feel curious to see it. Life itself being worth less, all things with it, which minister to it, are worth less. . . .

I walk toward one of our ponds; but what signifies the beauty of nature when men are base? We walk to lakes to see our serenity reflected in them; when we are not serene, we go not to them. Who can be serene in a country where both the rulers and the ruled are without principle? The remembrance of my country spoils my walk. My thoughts are murder to the State, and involuntarily go plotting against her.[81]

In this essay, Thoreau calls not only for the government of Massachusetts to protect its citizens, but also for individual citizens to follow the examples of those who had attacked the Boston Courthouse in response to the Fugitive Slave Law.[82] He asks citizens to withdraw their support to the state:

What should concern Massachusetts is not the Nebraska Bill, nor the Fugitive Slave Bill, but her own slaveholding and servility. Let the State dissolve her union with the slaveholder. She may wriggle and hesitate, and ask leave to read the Constitution once more; but she can find no respectable law or precedent that sanctions the continuance of such a union for an instant.

Let each inhabitant of the State dissolve his union with her, as long as she delays to do her duty.[83]

This essay also marks the first time that Thoreau used rhetoric that went beyond noncooperation to advocating revolt against the government, if necessary: "We have used up all our inherited freedom. If we would save our lives, we must fight for them."[84] From tone to tactics, the absolute faith in moral reform as a method of social reform gives way to a willingness to actively fight for social reform.

One of Thoreau's final essays, "A Plea for Captain John Brown," demonstrates the end of a marked shift in his ideas on social change, particularly as they relate to reformers, social action and violence. In this essay Thoreau champions John Brown as a model reformer and citizen, even comparing his actions to those of Christ.[85] He portrays Brown as the ideal citizen, who was willing to take immediate action in the midst of unjust law. In Thoreau's words, Brown was "the most American of us all" and a "superior man."[86] Brown was ready to resist injustice in any way possible, including taking a life or giving his own for the cause. In recognizing and praising Brown for this, the reader can see Thoreau's most radical change from his earlier attitudes on social reform; in the wake of unwavering government injustice Thoreau moved to reluctantly accept violence as a means of social change:

> I do not wish to kill nor be killed, but I can foresee circumstances in which both these things would be by me unavoidable. We preserve the so-called "peace" of our community by deeds of petty violence every day.[87]

> I think that for once the Sharp's rifles and the revolvers were employed in a righteous cause. The tools were in the hands of one who could use them.
> The question is not about the weapon, but the spirit in which you use it.[88]

Thoreau's attitudes on social reform can be traced from a focus on self-reform as a mechanism for broader social change, to individual action from principle and noncooperation, to a willingness to fight and use violence, if necessary, in order to achieve social change. This shift marked an acknowledgement that the individual could not enjoy and engage in self-cultivation in an environment where the individual conscience was trampled. Perhaps because Thoreau's ideas on social reform went through several variations, his works remain important to a range of activists, from contemplative monastics and pacifists to radical revolutionaries—a testament to his legacy as a writer and thinker.

Despite popular interpretations of Thoreau's work, he was not "antiprogress." In his analysis of society he remained deeply concerned with the social definition of progress, holding that broader ideals were ill conceived. Behind advances in economic well-being, technology, and science, he found illusions that prevented individuals from the true progress of personal development. Conventional ideals of progress—be they technological, economic, or scientific advance—often restricted the individual. He looked to other civilizations in his analysis to prove that "civilization" was a subjective term, and that many "savage" societies possessed a greater quality of life than modern America recognized. Thoreau's works continue to challenge readers worldwide to reconsider their own definitions of progress by exploring such concepts as consumer "needs," necessities of life, and poverty. Though his own views of progressive reform changed over time, his writings on this topic continue to inspire those who face social injustice.

Critiquing Thoreau's Social Analysis

At this point in the book it is prudent to briefly explore some of the potential limitations of Thoreau's social analysis. There are certainly a number of areas within his work that are vulnerable to critique. For those who believe social thought should not be wedded to moral imperatives, there is certainly room to attack Thoreau's work for its inherent ethical and humanist assumptions. While the value-neutral sociologist would make a clear delineation between the "ought" (preferred or ideal order) and the "is" (actual reality), Thoreau believed the distance between the two was simply a matter of individual action from principle, which was the duty of any moral citizen. Perhaps a more dire sociological error on Thoreau's part was his absolute faith in the power of the individual to resist social forces, as well as what some might call a "misguided" view of the practicality of individual reform. Furthermore, by twenty-first-century standards, Thoreau's view of economy, especially his ideas on economic "self-reliance," could certainly be categorized as out of touch with the economic realities of a global consumer culture. Along with his preference for economic self-sufficiency, Thoreau's dismissal of a complex division of labor could be viewed as over-romanticizing the "simple" life while downplaying the positive functions of a capitalist economy. In the final section of this chapter I will focus on the latter two of these aspects of Thoreau's work: his absolute faith in the individual and his preference for individual economic self-sufficiency.

The Individual versus Society

While more macro-oriented sociologists might recognize Thoreau for his analysis of the ways in which the material and structural realities of social life influenced the individual, they would certainly have good reason to turn a skeptical eye toward his romantic faith in the individual's ability to resist society and its institutions. Thoreau's overwhelming confidence in the individual's ability to "transcend" the limiting and negative forces of society, as well as his sometimes jaded portrayal of the relationship between the individual and society, could certainly be labeled as idealistic or naive. His attitude is not unlike that of a stubborn undergraduate student who resists the sociological perspective by insisting that the individual "should" be able to oppose social forces. Unlike many resistant students, though, Thoreau did recognize the reality of the social forces. He simply believed that they could and should be overcome by the individual. Indeed, he held the assumption that any individual, if awakened to the realities of society, could act to change things. Thoreau's view of social reform over-optimistically assumes that any and all individuals have the power to effect changes within broader social structures and organizations. This individualist bias in Thoreau's model of society is undeniable—the individual was the central unit Thoreau's social analysis. This was an approach that originated from his Transcendental view of the self—a standpoint that often bordered on deification of the individual.

While these biases in Thoreau's work could be viewed as sociological "shortcomings," there are several rejoinders that should keep us from overstating the weight of their critiques. Even though Thoreau's focus on the individual might overestimate individual agency in the midst of social life, readers often take these limitations to the logical extreme by assuming that Thoreau was seeking to do away with "society" as a concept or that he advocated a complete withdrawal from social life. Such interpretations are certainly erroneous. In his book *Henry Thoreau: A Life of the Mind* (1986), Robert Richardson Jr. helps to clarify Thoreau's view of society by pointing out that rather than a disinterest in society, Thoreau harbored a disappointment with it. Beginning with Thoreau's first writing on social life, an 1838 Harvard essay entitled "Society," Richardson explores how Thoreau sought to deconstruct traditional views of society by reversing the idea that "man was made for society."[89] Instead, in his typical individualist attitude, Thoreau suggested that perhaps "society was made for man." Indeed, as Richardson makes clear, Thoreau actually believed that it was human nature for individuals to come together in social groups. The main problem for Thoreau was that humans "have not associated, but only assembled." According to Richardson, Thoreau did not want less society; he wanted a society in which people associated in a more authentic manner.[90] Most importantly, Richardson clarifies what is an often mistaken view of Thoreau's work—Thoreau did not deny the importance of society. Rather, he downplayed "social determinism" and any other efforts to place blame of individual failure on an intangible "society."[91] In this respect *he is guilty of being microsociological, rather than nonsociological.* Indeed, his overwhelming emphasis on the individual is actually proximate to more microsociological theories, such as symbolic interactionism, which espouse confidence in the ability of the individual as a primary agent in shaping his or her own reality. The legacy of Thoreau's ideas on the power of the individual demonstrates that there is more practicality in his work than some critics might admit. There is little doubt that his philosophies of individual action from principle and individual civil disobedience have been the impetus for worldwide social reform of political, economic, and environmental varieties.

A Hermit-Poet in a Global Economy?

While many believe that Thoreau's critiques of the economy remain poignant in an American consumer culture that relies on a specialized division of labor, others might contend that his frank ideas on the capitalist marketplace are unsophisticated, antiquated, or even laughable. They might simply dismiss his perspective as the utopian thought of a pastoral poet. As a member of the Transcendental elite and a graduate of Harvard, it may even seem that Thoreau denounced industrial capitalism from a position of privilege. Undeniably, within the context of the twenty-first century, Thoreau's ideal of a more "self-reliant" economy presents a number of pragmatic questions of economic realism, including whether billions of people can simply rely on themselves for goods and services without some type of division of labor. In an economy where corporate profits are built on creating new demands and an ever-expanding consumer culture, many Americans might even find the suggestion that we "simplify" our lives to be anti-American. After all, entire American industries are built upon convincing consumers to do the opposite, thus increasing the ideals of standard of living. The complexities of modern life as well as the entrenched relationship between employment, status, and social interaction make Thoreau's mantra "simplify" a mere delusion to many. These critiques do not just take Thoreau's ideas to the logical extreme; they commit the error of throwing the proverbial baby out with the bath water by dismissing Thoreau's evaluation of American capitalism simply because they disapprove of his vision that there might be another alternative. By arguing that "there is no other way," such approaches exemplify the very deterministic thought that Thoreau himself railed against: "So thoroughly and sincerely are we compelled to live, reverencing our life, and denying the possibility of change. This is the only way, we say; but there are as many ways as there can be drawn radii from one centre."[92]

However, if we resist an extreme reading of Thoreau as someone who advocated "smashing capitalism" or who sought a "pastoral and agrarian revolution," and instead reexamine his own actions, we can get a better understanding of his overall economic critiques and what economic alternatives he sought. It is no secret that Thoreau had his own connections to industrial capitalism. His father was a pencil manufacturer. Henry David not only worked in the family business, but also helped his father perfect the new ways to construct pencils by mixing clay and graphite. In addition, Thoreau worked to establish himself as a writer, including a stint in New York, where he sought a wider audience for his work. He also sold his services as a land surveyor in the marketplace. While these facts may be surprising and even hypocritical to some, there is less incongruence between his words and his actions than there appears on the surface. Beyond popular cultural views and created myths about Thoreau lies the heart of his argument: Quality of life does not equate with an arbitrary material standard of living. To be sure, Thoreau was no luddite seeking a nostalgic return to the past while denying the possibilities of the future. Instead, he looked for humans to create a better way of life, one that combined the best of the past with the best of what contemporary humanity had to offer. He certainly sought an alternative economic system that would maximize individual freedom and quality of life—both characteristics he believed were absent in the industrial capitalist system. And while he may appear to be an armchair economist to some, his ideas about the relationship of standard of living and quality of life are vindicated by a number of contemporary scholars who have demonstrated that standard of living and quality of life are not always correlated, and that our obsession with status and choices can actually decrease our personal happiness.[93] In this respect he is in agreement with one of the foremost economic theorists of his time, Karl Marx, and he was well ahead of the social critics of consumer culture that would emerge in the latter part of the twentieth century.

Notes

1. As pointed out by Laura Dassow Walls in *Seeing New Worlds: Henry David Thoreau and Nineteenth-Century Natural Science* (Madison: University of Wisconsin Press, 1995), 189, and Max Oelschlaeger in *The Idea of Wilderness: From Prehistory to the Age of Ecology* (New Haven, CT: Yale University Press, 1991), 149, Thoreau was already exploring speciation and patterns of change in forest communities prior to reading Darwin's *Origin of Species* (1860). For in-depth examination of Thoreau's evolution as a naturalist see both of the above-named texts and Robert Richardson Jr.'s *Henry Thoreau: A Life of the Mind* (Berkeley and Los Angeles: University of California Press, 1986).

2. See Oelschlaeger, *The Idea of Wilderness*, 139; and Fredrick Turner, *Natural Classicism: Essays on Literature and Science* (New York: Paragon, 1985), 173, 191. Turner argues that Thoreau wanted to use the pre-social as a method of understanding social reality.

3. Henry David Thoreau, "Walden," in *The Portable Thoreau*, rev. ed., ed. Carl Bode (New York: Penguin, 1987), 286–87.

4. Thoreau, "Walden," 267–68.

5. Thoreau, "Walden," 284–86.

6. Thoreau, "Walden," 285.

7. Thoreau, "Walden," 289–90.

8. Thoreau, "Walden," 269–70.

9. Thoreau, "Walden," 261.

10. Henry David Thoreau, "Life without Principle," in *The Portable Thoreau*, rev. ed., ed. Carl Bode (New York: Penguin, 1987), 652.

11. Thoreau states in "Walden," 306–307, "Our inventions are wont to be pretty toys, which distract our attention from serious things. They are but improved means to an unimproved end."

12. For example, in "Walden," 270–71, Thoreau asks, "What does he want next? Surely he does not want more warmth of the same kind, as more and richer food, larger and more splendid houses, finer and more abundant clothing and more numerous incessant and hotter fires, and the like. When he has obtained those things which are necessary to life, there is another alternative than to obtain the superfluities; and that is, to adventure on life now, his vacation from humbler toil having commenced."

13. Thoreau, "Walden," 310–11.

14. Thoreau, "Walden," 287–88.

15. Thoreau, "Walden," 263.

16. In "Walden," 268, Thoreau explores the possibilities of combining the best of both worlds: "So, we are told, the New Hollander goes naked with impunity, while the European shivers in his clothes. Is it possible to combine the hardiness of these savages with the intellectualness of the civilized man?" He goes on in "Walden," 286–87, to discuss housing: "He must have spent half of his life before his wigwam will be earned. Nevertheless, this points to an important distinction between the civilized man and the savage; and, no doubt, they have designs on us for our benefit, in making the life of a civilized people an institution, in which the life of an individual is to a great extent absorbed, in order to preserve and perfect that of the race. But I wish to show at what a sacrifice this advantage is at present obtained, and to suggest that we may possibly so live as to secure all the advantage without suffering any of the disadvantage."

17. Thoreau, "Walden," 421.

18. Thoreau, "Walden," 292.

19. See "Walden," 322, where Thoreau states: "The customs of some savage nations might, perchance, be profitably imitated by us, for at least they go through the semblance of casting their slough annually; they have the idea of a thing, whether they have the reality of it or not. Would it not be well if we were to celebrate such a 'busk,' or 'feast fruits,' as Bartram describes to have been the custom of the Mucclassee Indians? 'When a town celebrates the busk,' says he, 'having previously provided themselves with new clothes, new pots, pans, and other household utensils and furniture, they collect all of their worn out clothes and other despicable things, sweep and clean their houses, squares, and the whole town of their filth, which with all the remaining grain and older provisions they cast into one common heap and consume it with fire."

20. Thoreau, "Walden," 269–70.

21. Henry David Thoreau, "Walking," in *The Portable Thoreau*, rev. ed., ed. Carl Bode (New York: Penguin, 1987), 609.

22. Oelschlaeger, *The Idea of Wilderness*, 165.

23. Thoreau, "Walking," 614.

24. L. L. Bernard and Jessie Bernard, *The Origins of American Sociology: The Social Science Movement in the United States* (New York: Russell and Russell, 1965), 141.

25. George Ritzer, "Herbert Spencer," in *Classical Sociological Theory*, 3rd. ed. (Boston: McGraw-Hill, 2000), 121.

26. Ritzer, "Herbert Spencer," 125.

27. Ritzer, "Herbert Spencer," 121.

28. Lewis A. Coser, *Masters of Sociological Thought: Ideas in Historical and Social Context*, 2nd ed. (Fort Worth, TX: Harcourt Brace Jovanovich, 1977), 129–32.

29. Coser, *Masters of Sociological Thought*, 132–36.

30. See Thoreau, "Walden," 291–92, 308.

31. Thoreau, "Walden," 307.

32. Walls, *Seeing New Worlds*, 8.

33. Laura Dassow Walls, "The Man Most Alive," in *Material Faith: Henry David Thoreau on Science*, ed. Laura Dassow Walls and Parker Huber (Boston: Houghton Mifflin, 1999), ix.

34. Walls, "The Man Most Alive," xi.

35. In his *Journal of Henry David Thoreau*, ed. Bradford Torrey and Francis Allen (Boston: Houghton Mifflin, 1906), VI: 200, Thoreau writes: "It is remarkable how the American mind runs to statistics. Consider the number of meteorological observers and other annual phenomena. The Smithsonian Institution is truly a national institution. Every shopkeeper makes a record of the arrival of the first martin or bluebird to his box. Dodd, the broker, told me last spring that he knew when the first bluebird came to his box. . . . Beside so many entries in their day-books and ledgers, they record these things."

36. Richardson, *Henry Thoreau*, 381.

37. Walls, "The Man Most Alive," xiv.

38. Richardson, *Henry Thoreau*, 363.

39. Robert Richardson Jr., "Thoreau and Science," in *American Literature and Science*, ed. Robert Scholnik (Lexington: University Press of Kentucky, 1992), 110–27.

40. Walls, *Seeing New Worlds*, 8.

41. Thoreau argues in *Journal 4: 1851–1852*, ed. Leonard Neufeldt and Nancy Craig Simmons (Princeton, NJ: Princeton University Press, 1992), 221–23, that science would harness human knowledge: "What sort of science is that which enriches the understanding but robs the imagination. . . . That is simply the way in which it speaks to the understanding and that is the account which the understanding gives it—but that is not the way it speaks to the Imagination & that is not the account which the Imagination gives it. Just as inadequate to a pure mechanic would be a poet's account of a steam engine. . . . If we knew all things thus mechanically merely should we know anything really?"

42. Oelschlaeger, *The Idea of Wilderness*, 158.

43. Thoreau, in *Journal*, X: 293–95.

44. Oelschlaeger, *The Idea of Wilderness*, 143.

45. Oelschlaeger, *The Idea of Wilderness*, 158

46. Thoreau, in *Journal*, XIII: 29–30.

47. Thoreau, in *Journal*, XI: 358–60.

48. Thoreau also believed that humans would degenerate from a proper relationship with nature to a scientific, mechanical interaction.

49. Thoreau, in *Journal*, VI: 236–38.

50. For example, Thoreau states in *Journal 2: 1842–1848*, ed. Robert Sattelmeyer (Princeton, NJ: Princeton University Press, 1984), 91: "Many a book has been written which does necessarily suggest or imply the phenomenon or object which it professes to have been written. But we may begin anywhere within nature. Strictly speaking, there is no such thing as an elementary knowledge. There is always a chasm between knowledge and ignorance which the steps of science can never pass."

51. In the essay "Walking," 623, Thoreau states: "My desire for knowledge is intermittent, but my desire to bathe my head in atmospheres unknown to my feet is perennial and constant. The highest that we can attain to is not Knowledge, but Sympathy with Intelligence. I do not know that this higher knowledge amounts to anything more definite than a novel and grand surprise on a sudden revelation of the insufficiency of all that we call Knowledge before,—a discovery that there are more things in heaven and earth than are dreamed of in our philosophy. It is the lighting up of the mist by the sun. Man cannot know in any higher sense than this."

52. Thoreau, *Journal*, XII: 371.

53. Thoreau, *Journal*, XIII: 168–69.

54. Thoreau, *Journal*, XII: 371.

55. Thoreau *Journal*, XIII: 180–81.

56. Richardson, *Henry Thoreau*, 374–76.

57. See Walls, *Seeing New Worlds*, 4. In *A Week on the Concord and Merrimack Rivers*, ed. Carl Hovde, William Howarth, and Elizabeth Hall Witherall (Princeton, NJ: Princeton University Press, 1980), 361–66, Thoreau states, "He is not a true man of science who does bring some sympathy to his studies, and expect to learn something by behavior as well as by application. It is childish to rest in the discoveries of mere coincidences, or of partial extraneous laws. . . .

"The poet uses the results of science and philosophy, and generates their widest deductions."

58. See Walls, "The Man Most Alive," xiii. An example of Thoreau's thoughts on using poetry, philosophy and science can be found in *Journal*, VIII: 314–16: "Again, as so many times, I [am] reminded of the advantage of the poet, and philosopher, and naturalist, and whomsoever, of pursuing from time to time some other business than his chosen one,—seeing with the side of his eye. The poet will so get visions which no deliberate abandonment can secure. The philosopher is so forced to recognize principles which long study might not detect. And the naturalist even will stumble upon some new and unexpected flower or animal. . . ."

59. Carl Bode, "Introduction," in *The Portable Thoreau*, rev. ed., ed. Carl Bode (New York: Penguin, 1987). 1-27.

60. Thoreau, *Journal*, XI: 153.

61. Thoreau, *Journal 4*, 356–57.

62. See Henry David Thoreau, "Excursions," in *The Writings of Henry David Thoreau* (Boston: Houghton Mifflin, 1893), 9: 160–62. In addition, Richardson points out in *Henry Thoreau*, 356, that Thoreau's travels with Joe Polis, a Penobscot Indian, along with his other research on American Indians, led him to believe that the scientist had a lot to learn from American Indians about "observational acuity."

63. See Oelschlaeger, *The Idea of Wilderness*, 139. For an example of this in Thoreau's writing see "Walking," 622–23, where he argues that science was a harness to human knowledge: "What we call knowledge is often our positive ignorance; ignorance our negative knowledge. By long years of patient industry and reading of the newspapers,—for what are the libraries of science but files of newspapers?—a man accumulates a myriad facts, lays them up in his memory, and then when in some spring of his life he saunters abroad into the great Fields of thought, he as it were goes to grass like a horse, and leaves all his harness behind in the stable."

64. See Oelschlaeger, *The Idea of Wilderness*, 139. Oelschlaeger points out that "Indian wisdom" allowed Thoreau to break free from the limits of conventional wisdom, which used standardized ways of thought.

65. Walls, *Seeing New Worlds*, 4, 8.

66. Leonard Gougeon, "Thoreau and Reform," in *The Cambridge Companion to Henry David Thoreau*, ed. Joel Myerson (New York: Cambridge University Press, 1995), 196.

67. Thoreau makes a number of observations about reformers and philanthropists in "Walden," including the following on pages 329–332: "I never heard of a philanthropic meeting in which it was sincerely proposed to do any good to me of the like of me. . . .

"Philanthropy is almost the only virtue which is sufficiently appreciated by mankind. Nay, it is greatly overrated; and it is our selfishness which overrates it. . . .

"His goodness must not be a partial and transitory act, but a constant superfluity, which costs him nothing and of which he is unconscious. . . .

"I believe that what so saddens the reformer is not his sympathy with his fellows in distress, but, though he be the holiest son of God, is his private ail."

68. Thoreau, "Walden," 327.

69. Thoreau, "Walden," 328.

70. Henry David Thoreau, "Paradise (to be) Regained," in *Reform Papers: The Writings of Henry D. Thoreau*, ed. Wendell Glick (Princeton, NJ: Princeton University Press, 1973), 42.

71. Thoreau speaks of the need for inner moral reform in "Paradise (to be) Regained," 45–46: "Undoubtedly if we were to reform this outward life truly and thoroughly, we should find no duty of the inner omitted. It would be employment for our whole nature; and what we should do there-after would be as vain a question as to ask the bird what it will do when its nest is built and its brood reared. But a moral re-

form must take place first, and then the necessity of the other will be superseded, and we shall sail and plough by its force alone."

72. Gougen, "Thoreau and Reform," 198.

73. Gougen, "Thoreau and Reform," 200.

74. Gougen, "Thoreau and Reform," 202.

75. For example, in "Civil Disobedience," in *The Portable Thoreau*, rev. ed., ed. Carl Bode (New York: Penguin, 1987), 132, Thoreau argues: "Why expose yourself to this overwhelming brute force? You do not resist cold and hunger, the winds and the waves, thus obstinately; you quietly submit to a thousand similar necessities. You do not put your head into the fire. But just in proportion as I regard this as not wholly a brute force, but partly a human force, and consider that I have relations to those millions as to so many millions of men, and not of mere brute or inanimate things, I see that appeal is possible, first and instantaneously, from them to the Maker of them, and, secondly, from them to themselves. But, if I put my head deliberately into the fire . . . I have only myself to blame. . . . And, above all, there is this difference between resisting this and a purely brute or natural force, that I can resist this with some effect; but I cannot expect, like Orpheus, to change the nature of the rocks and trees and beasts."

76. Thoreau's language in "Civil Disobedience" does show a change in tone from his previous work. For example, on pages 119–120 he states: "If the injustice is part of the necessary friction of the machine of government, let it go, let it go; perchance it will wear smooth—certainly the machine will wear out. If the injustice has a spring, or a pulley, or a rope, or a crank, exclusively for itself, then perhaps you may consider whether the remedy will not be worse than the evil; but if it is of such a nature that it requires you to be the agent of injustice to another, then, I say, break the law. Let your life be a counter friction to stop the machine. What I have to do is to see, at any rate, that I do not lend myself to the wrong which I condemn." He invokes the idea of action from principle on pages 118–19: "How can a man be satisfied to entertain an opinion merely, and enjoy *it?* Is there any enjoyment in it, if his opinion is that he is aggrieved? If you are cheated out of a single dollar by your neighbor, you do not rest satisfied with knowing that you are cheated, or with saying that you are cheated, or even with petitioning him to pay you your due; but you take effectual steps at once to obtain the full amount, and see that you are never cheated again. Action from principle—the perception and the performance of right—changes things and relations; it is essentially revolutionary, and does not consist wholly with anything which was. It not only divides states and churches, it divides families; ay, it divides the *individual*, separating the diabolical in him from the divine."

77. Thoreau, "Civil Disobedience," 113–14.

78. Gougen, "Thoreau and Reform," 205.

79. Thoreau states in "Slavery in Massachusetts," in *Reform Papers: The Writings of Henry D. Thoreau*, ed. Wendell Glick (Princeton, NJ: Princeton University Press, 1973), 94–95: "The whole military force of the State is at the service of a Mr. Suttle,

a slaveholder from Virginia, to enable him to catch a man whom he calls his property; but not a soldier is offered to save a citizen of Massachusetts from being kidnapped! Is this what all these soldiers, all this *training*, have been for these seventy-nine years past? Have they been trained merely to rob Mexico and carry back fugitive slaves to their masters?"

80. Gougen, "Thoreau and Reform," 205.

81. Thoreau, "Slavery in Massachusetts," 106–108.

82. Gougen, "Thoreau and Reform," 204.

83. Thoreau, "Slavery in Massachusetts," 104.

84. Thoreau, "Slavery in Massachusetts," 108.

85. Thoreau's words canonized John Brown throughout the essay "A Plea for Captain John Brown," in *Reform Papers: The Writings of Henry D. Thoreau*, ed. Wendell Glick (Princeton, NJ: Princeton University Press, 1973): "He was firmer and higher principled than any that I have chanced to hear of as there" (113).

"You who pretend to care for Christ crucified, consider what you are about to do to him who offered himself to be the savior of four millions of men. . . . Some eighteen hundred years ago Christ was crucified; this morning, perchance, Captain Brown was hung. These are the two ends of a chain which is not without its links" (136).

"I speak for the slave when I say, that I prefer the philanthropy of Captain John Brown to that Philanthropy which neither shoots me nor liberates me" (133).

"When the time came, few men were found willing to lay down their lives in defense of what they knew to be wrong. They did not like that this should be their last act in this world" (117).

"He was a superior man. He did not value his bodily life in comparison with ideal things. He did not recognize unjust human laws, but resisted them as he was bid. . . . In that sense he was the most American of us all" (125).

"I hear many condemn these men because they were so few. When were the good and brave ever in the majority? Would you have had him wait till that time came?—till you and I came over him? The very fact that he had no rabble or troop of hirelings about him would alone distinguish him from ordinary heroes. His company was small indeed, because few could be found worthy to pass his muster. Each one who there laid down his life for the poor and oppressed, was a picked man, called out of many thousands, if not millions; apparently a man of principle, of rare courage and devoted humanity, ready to sacrifice his life at any moment for the benefits of his fellow man. . . . These alone were ready to step between the oppressed and the oppressor" (131–32).

86. Thoreau, "A Plea for Captain John Brown," 125.

87. Thoreau, "A Plea for Captain John Brown," 133.

88. Thoreau, "A Plea for Captain John Brown," 133.

89. Richardson, *Henry Thoreau*, 31.

90. Richardson, *Henry Thoreau*, 33.

91. Richardson, *Henry Thoreau*, 34.

92. Thoreau, "Walden," 266–67.

93. See Richard Layard, *Happiness: Lessons from a New Science* (New York: Penguin, 2005); Tim Kasser, *The High Price of Materialism* (Cambridge, MA: MIT Press, 2003); Barry Schwartz, *The Paradox of Choice: Why More Is Less* (New York: Harper Perennial, 2005).

CHAPTER FIVE

~

Thoreau's Social Inquiry

No method nor discipline can supersede the necessity of being forever on the alert. What is a course of history or philosophy, or poetry, no matter how well selected, or the best society, or the most admirable routine of life, compared with the discipline of looking always at what is to be seen? Will you be a reader, a student merely, or a seer? Read your fate, see what is before you, and walk on into futurity.[1]

Thoreau did not simply ask sociological questions. He went about examining these questions in ways that were more sociological than many scholars have previously acknowledged. In fact, if we examine Thoreau's approach to looking at society, as well as his intentions for writing, we can see parallels to the role of the public sociologist. The posthumous recognition of Thoreau as an important public intellectual lies in his ability to awaken readers, a mission that aligns him closely with sociology. By questioning authority and examining the effect of society on the individual, Thoreau aimed to allow readers to see their own society with new eyes. Yet he also made efforts to open the reader to "seeing" other cultures and values. From social class to social savage, he exposed readers to other ways of living and behaving, as well as to positions not typically taken into account by mainstream American values. In this chapter we will move beyond the ways in which Thoreau's background and themes relate to sociology, to explore the objectives and inquiry that fueled his writing.

"Awakening"

Just as sociologists aim to open the windows of daily social life, Thoreau attempted to *see beyond the ordinary*, with an altered and more deliberate perception. In his search to see with "new eyes," he mastered perspective by looking at common things in an uncommon manner.[2] From his prolonged use of Walden Pond as a "laboratory" to his adoption of the vantage point of prisoner for "Civil Disobedience," he constantly stepped outside the framework of mainstream consciousness by refusing to live according to conventional social expectations.[3] Thoreau was adept at inverting his vision to see all phenomena—nature, the individual, and society—in a new way. For anyone to see the "least fact or phenomenon, however familiar," in a new way, he argued in his journal, all they needed to do was observe it "from a point a hair's breadth aside from our habitual path or routine."[4] Having experienced the exhilaration of this awakening, Thoreau believed he had transcended his own slumber and possessed an elevated consciousness that allowed him to see through the illusions of society: "The greater part of what my neighbors call good I believe in my soul to be bad, and if I repent anything, it is very likely to be my good behavior. . . . —I hear an irresistible voice that invites me away from all that."[5] "No method nor discipline," he writes in *Walden*, "can supersede the necessity of being forever on the alert."[6] Though he remained dedicated to the subjective experience, Thoreau regularly attempted to see from outside himself:

> With thinking we may be beside ourselves in a sane sense. By a conscious effort of the mind we can stand aloof from actions and their consequences; and all good things, good and bad, go by us like a torrent. . . . I only know myself as a human entity; the scene, so to speak, of thoughts and affections; and am sensible of a certain doubleness by which I can stand as remote from myself as another. However intense my experience, I am conscious of the presence and criticism of a part of me, which, as it were, is not a part of me, but spectator, sharing no experience, but taking note of it; and that is no more I than it is you.[7]

This perspective also remains a central objective of sociology—to "think oneself away" momentarily in order to see through the illusions of society, hold a clearer picture of social realities, and behold the influences society exacted on the individual, devoid of any bias. We can find congruence, then, in Thoreau's "awakening" and the task of sociology in everyday life. This semblance becomes even more apparent if we look at his methods and objectives as a writer.

Beyond his own view, Thoreau wanted to *awaken the reader*, unveil her sight and allow her to see with new eyes the illusions and self-emptiness created by modern life.[8] He often argued in his writing that this reawakening was necessary, since most Americans lived their lives in perpetual slumber:

> The millions are awake enough for physical labor; but only one in a million is awake enough for effective intellectual exertion, only one in a hundred millions to a poetic or divine life. To be awake is to be alive. I have never yet met a man who was quite awake.[9]

Thoreau elaborated on his ideas of daily inquiry by addressing one of his first rules of "seeing," which is also one of the first great rules of sociology: things are not what they seem. In *Walden*, for example, he argues that New Englanders lived as they did because their vision "did not penetrate the surface of things."[10] Very few truly gazed toward reality with the intention of understanding it. If they did, they would be better equipped to stand apart from the influence of institutions such as the economic system, and they would be more likely to live as autonomous individuals. In his role as a social observer, Thoreau concerned himself with the ways that humans confirmed and condoned their daily routines through self-deception; as a writer and public intellectual, he strove to demonstrate that these illusions were often accepted as the "soundest truth," even though they were really petty concerns:

> Shams and delusions are esteemed for soundest truths, while reality is fabulous. If men would steadily observe realities only, and not allow themselves to be deluded, life, to compare it with such things as we know, would be like a fairy tale and the Arabian Nights' Entertainments. . . . When we are unhurried and wise, we perceive that only the great and worthy things have any permanent and absolute existence,—that petty fears and petty pleasures are but the shadow of reality. This is always exhilarating and sublime. By *closing the eyes and slumbering, and consenting to be deceived by shows, men establish and confirm their daily life of routine and habit everywhere, which is still built on purely illusory foundations.*[11]

If we specifically examine the italicized part of this passage we find a striking similarity to the "debunking" mentality of sociology described by Peter Berger in his classical explorations of sociological consciousness, *An Invitation to Sociology*:

> The sociological frame of reference, with its built-in procedure of looking for levels of reality other than those given in the official interpretation's of society, carries with it a logical imperative *to unmask the pretentions and the propaganda by which men cloak their actions with each other.*[12]

Thoreau, like sociologists such as Berger, sought ways to unveil to the public how humans condone and cloak their activities with deception. Berger equates this new form of consciousness to satori, "the experience of illumination sought in Zen Buddhism," and describes it as "seeing things with new eyes."[13] Likewise, for Thoreau this awakening was a new and ultimate form of liberty. Seeing would allow the reader to understand and reject self and social deception, and to live a more authentic life.

"Seeing beyond the Verge of Sight"

Thoreau's interest in the idea of awakening, like other social critics and many sociologists, led him to *examine and question many of the commonly accepted goals* that Americans blindly pursued and to *analyze the meanings behind human behavior*. From the economic goals of work and consumption that we discussed in chapter 3 to the ambitions of modern progress reviewed in chapter 4, Thoreau sought to explore the illusions and realities behind American ideals. He pointed out to the reader the hidden meaning and consequences of market activities by discussing the ways in which capitalist ethos attributed different values to objects and individuals, and the ensuing stratification that resulted. He explored the meanings that were attached to people and objects as outward characteristics became symbolic of interior qualities. He recognized how fashion became a fetish and the ways in which material goods were increasingly used to symbolize class and status. Thoreau also examined the role of power in society by turning his analysis to authority figures such as the United States government. He not only questioned the process by which government officials were selected, but also the motives behind their actions and policies. Thoreau's awakening, then, did not beckon citizens to simply look at the complexities of nature, but to examine the complexities of their own lives and culture by engaging in an in-depth exploration of social meanings, power, and ideals.

Beyond analysis of his own society, though, Thoreau also made attempts to *"see" other cultures, classes, and idea systems*. He was open to the intellectual voyage of learning about other ways of living and behaving, and he was anxious to shrug off the confinement and provincialism of nineteenth-century America, which he believed was far too ethnocentric. Individuals needed to look to all learned societies for inspiration and cultural enrichment:

> If we live in the Nineteenth Century, why should we not enjoy the advantages that the Nineteenth Century offers? Why should our life be in any respect

provincial? If we will read newspapers, why not skip the gossip of Boston and take the best newspaper in the world at once?—not be sucking the pap of "neutral family" papers, or browsing "Olive Branches" here in New England. Let the reports of all the learned societies come to us, and we will see if they know anything. Why should we leave it to Harper & Brothers and Redding & Co. to select our reading? As the nobleman of cultivated taste surrounds himself with whatever conduces to his culture—genius—learning—wit—books—paintings—statuary—music—philosophical instruments, and the like.[14]

With respect to a true culture and manhood, we are essentially provincial still, not metropolitan—mere Jonathans. We are provincial, because we do not find at home our standards, because we do not worship truth, but the reflection of truth, because we are warped and narrowed by an exclusive devotion to trade and commerce and manufacturing and agriculture and the like, which are but means, and not the end.[15]

A distaste for provincialism and a desire to transcend the expectations of his own society led Thoreau to explore a number of other cultural lifestyles. He sought out new and unknown worlds, particularly with regard to knowledge and daily living. The entire Walden experiment was a tribute to the alternative lifestyles he valued in other societies, with their simplicity and self-reliance, rather than a capitalistic clock measured day. He was able to live at Walden free of many mainstream social expectations and goals, including the ideals of holding well-paying and respectable employment, or owning and maintaining a sizable house.

Beyond the Walden experiment, though, Thoreau also conducted in-depth studies into the cultures of American Indians. In A Week on the Concord and Merrimack Rivers, he examines "red-white" relations in New England and his ideas on how these relations could progress.[16] The Maine Woods chronicles Thoreau's three excursions (1846, 1853, and 1857) into the Maine wilderness and includes his accounts of traveling with his guide, Joe Polis, a Penobscot Indian.[17] At the time of his death Thoreau had amassed more than eleven notebooks, totaling over twenty-eight hundred pages of extracts and commentary from books about the American Indian.[18] Robert Richardson Jr., author of Henry Thoreau: A Life of the Mind, points out that Thoreau avoided more popular works in his research into American Indians; instead, he examined more than 270 sources, including The Jesuit Relations, a document that focused on habits, customs, manners, language, clothing, behavior, beliefs, and history.[19] Richardson believes that Thoreau took from these sources, which also included Herman Melville's Typee (1846), a recognition that cultural differences were not only relative, but that outside observers often gave accounts of native cultures that portrayed them as backward and uncivilized.[20] Aside from his compendium of secondary information on American Indians, Thoreau was able to observe them on a few occasions, taking simple notes from his own observations on activities such as cooking methods and the construction of animal traps.[21] Lawrence Buell, author of *The Environmental Imagination*, points out that over the course of his research, Thoreau's view of American Indian culture progressed from a romanticized image to an appreciation of its simplicity of lifestyle and its ability to read and express the natural environment.[22] He was the first major Anglo-American creative writer, Buell argues, to recognize native cultures as a model for environmental perception.[23] Robert Sayre, author of *Thoreau and the American Indians*, points out that few other Americans had come so far in their view of the American Indian.[24] Not only was Thoreau's interest in the American Indian based on his historical and somewhat anthropological fascination, as Sayre states, but Thoreau's exploration of the American Indian provided him with a point from which to criticize American culture.[25]

Thoreau's journals show that he read widely about other societies, from travel accounts of Granada and Columbia to the sacred texts of Asia. Over the course of his lifetime he read a large number of Eastern works, including translations of the Laws of Menu, Zendavesta, Hindustan, philosophy of the ancient Hindoos, Mahabarata, Vishnu Purana, Sama Veda, and four Upanishads. Richardson notes that Thoreau was deeply moved by the Laws of Menu and the Vishna Purana, and that these works supported Thoreau's ideas of awakening, individual freedom, and liberation.[26] Richardson also argues that Thoreau's interest in sacred Eastern works demonstrated that he did not see the Bible-centered Judeo-Christian worldview as the only or most accurate account of the universe.[27] Perhaps more than any other American writer, Thoreau was not a citizen of one society, but of many. "No place could ever be strange to me again," he writes in *Walden*.[28] He yearned for new horizons of human possibility, and he used many avenues to find them, including his readings, his fascination with American Indian culture, and his experiment at Walden Pond.

With such a strong fascination with other cultures, it should come as no surprise that Thoreau recognized and made efforts to *examine the relativity of cultural values*. He looked to his own society as well as other civilizations, to demonstrate that values and definitions were different depending on a number of historical and cultural factors. In his immediate environment he critiqued the values that emerged from the American economic system. The capitalist ethos provided a total interpretation of reality in America by structuring all aspects of life—nature, time, physical space, status, and human interaction. This system of meaning also had forces of countering deviance, which Thoreau examined in his discussions of fashion and consumption. He also recognized that human observation was relative to the language system of the society being examined. He engaged in an internal dialogue over this issue through his fascination with the language of science and measurement, as well as his exploration of the language systems of American Indians. As was discussed in chapter 4, Thoreau used the issue of development as a means to examine the variation of values across time and physical location. He made special efforts to deconstruct the relative definitions of "progress," "poverty," and "civilized." It is this comparative view and deconstruction of traditional American ideals that has spoken to so many readers who are as eager as Thoreau was to possess a broader view of reality than is afforded through the lens of only one culture.

We can see examples of Thoreau's interest in testing relative values and his *examination of segments of society outside of the mainstream* if we look at those with whom Thoreau associated. It is true that Thoreau was a graduate of Harvard, and that he kept company with Emerson, who had garnered prestige and popularity. However, Thoreau made efforts to regularly interact in meaningful ways, either at Walden or in his daily travels, with individuals who fell outside the "worthy" or "proper" segment of society.[29] These visitors came from all walks of life, and included women, children, railroad workers, farmers, the "old and infirm," a slave, the poor, and loggers. It was in the lesser-valued visitors and acquaintances that Thoreau found interest and worth. Though society ignored these individuals, he noted their peculiarities and argued that there was much to be learned from their experiences. He found many of them to be wiser than the town leaders. For example, when Thoreau discussed three separate visitors he hosted at Walden—the elderly dame, the pauper, and the woodchopper—he noted that despite their invisibility to the rest of society, they were sincere, free of the social disease that had come over most citizens, and capable of engaging in a wondrous exchange. They had not been shaped and formed by the ways of the capitalist society, which meant that they were more capable of thinking for themselves. Such experiences led Thoreau to suggest that there may be other "men of genius" to be found in the "lower grades of life."[30]

One of Thoreau's most transformative experiences of other classes of society came during the night he spent in jail for not paying the poll tax. His account of this event demonstrates his interest in observing the structure, activities, and inmates of the jail from a neutral position. In "Civil Disobedience" he equates the experience with traveling into a far country.

He also points out that a change came over his eyes after that night, and that many in his society were not even aware that such a place existed in their town. Thoreau's openness to take on a vantage point outside of the mainstream is quite evident from the following passage:

> The night in prison was novel and interesting enough. . . .
> It was like traveling into a far country, such as I had never expected to behold, to lie there for one night. It seemed to me that I never had heard the town-clock strike before, nor the evening sounds of the village; for we slept with the windows open. . . . It was to see my native village in the light of the middle ages. . . . I was an involuntary spectator and auditor of whatever was done and said in the kitchen of the adjacent village-inn,—a wholly new and rare experience to me. It was a closer view of my native town. I was fairly inside of it. I never had seen its institutions before. This is one of its peculiar institutions. . . . I began to comprehend what its inhabitants were all about. . . .
> When I came out of prison— . . . a change had to my eyes come over the scene,—the town and State, and country,—greater than any that mere time could effect. I saw yet more distinctly the State in which I lived. I saw to what extent the people among whom I lived could be trusted as good neighbors and friends; . . . that they did not greatly propose to do right; . . . for I believe that many of them are not aware that they have such an institution as the jail in their village.[31]

During his stay, Thoreau made an effort to get as much information from his fellow prisoner as he could. He became an "involuntary spectator," taking in the activity of the night in the village and learning an informal history through the writings of former prisoners. He saw this experience as a "closer view" of his town than he had previously possessed. This new vantage point changed Thoreau by allowing him to see more clearly the state in which he lived.

Thoreau also explored other landscapes outside of mainstream American culture, as well as those who dwelled there. For example, he spent time traveling in the Maine woods, especially near the lumber camps that were perched along the rivers. He described this land, "just up the river," as grim, savage, and dreary. It was a different world from the "civilization" of Thoreau's eighteenth-century American—certainly not the geographical region of the proper citizen. The inhabitants of this land were even more fascinating to Thoreau. On his first trip, in 1846, he traveled with loggers up the Penobscot. During this excursion he spent time at the logging camps, experiencing life in the wild, while learning about the work and leisure of the loggers. In *The Maine Woods*, he describes the campsites, food, and working conditions:

These camps were about twenty feet long by fifteen wide, built of logs—hemlock, cedar, spruce or yellow birch—one kind alone, or all together, with the bark on; . . . usually the scenery about them is drear and savage enough; and the logger's camp is as completely in the woods as a fungus at the foot of a pine in the swamp; no outlook but to the sky overhead; . . . the logger's fare consists of tea, molasses, flour, pork,—sometimes beef,—and beans.[32]

We filed into the rude loggers' camp at this place. . . . On the well flattened and somewhat faded beds . . . lay an odd leaf of the Bible, some genealogical chapter out of the Old Testament; . . . and we found Emerson's Address on the West India Emancipation which had been left here formerly by one of our company . . . and an odd number of the Westminster Review. . . . This was the readable, or reading matter, in a lumberer's camp in the Maine woods. . . . These things were well thumbed and soiled.[33]

Other than the food and reading material, Thoreau points out that the loggers had few amenities. Aside from the primitive environment, he described the lifestyle as solitary and the work as dangerous business. His description of the lengths to which the loggers went to drive the logs down the river reads not like that of a wanderlustful poet, but more like a foreign travel correspondent. In fact, excerpts of section 1 of The Maine Woods, "Ktaadn, and the Maine Woods," which first appeared in the Union magazine (1848), were also published by Horace Greeley in the New York Tribune. These passages from the earlier parts of the manuscript demonstrate not only the acute description that is customary of Thoreau's writing, but also a profound sense of fascination with the lifestyle of the loggers:

It was easy to see that driving logs must be an exciting as well as arduous and dangerous business. . . . They have quite an alphabet of their own, which only the practised can read. One of my companions read off from his memorandum book some marks of his own logs, among which there were crosses, belts, crow's feet, girdles . . . and various other devices. . . . The boys along the shore learn to walk on floating logs as city boys walk on sidewalks. Sometimes the logs are thrown up on rocks . . . or they jam together at rapids or falls, and accumulate in vast piles, which the driver must start at the risk of his life. Such is the lumber business, which depends on many accidents.[34]

I will describe particularly how we got over some of these portages and rapids, in order that the reader may get an idea of the boatman's life. At Ambejijis Falls, for instance, there was the roughest path imaginable cut through the woods; at first up the hill at an angle of nearly forty-five degrees, over rocks and logs without end. . . . Our two men at length took the batteau upon their shoulders, and, while two of us steadied it, to prevent it from rocking and wearing into their shoulders, on which they placed their hats folded, walked bravely over the remaining distance, with two or three pauses. . . . With this crushing weight they must climb and stumble along over fallen trees and slippery rocks of all sizes.[35]

Thoreau was certainly charmed with this lifestyle, which combined his ideals of learning nature and its ways, living on the boundaries of the primitive, and even a new language—the logger's "alphabet." Though they lived outside "civilization," Thoreau concluded that they had advanced minds:

> If I were to look for a narrow, uninformed, and countrified mind, as opposed to the intelligence and refinement which are thought to emanate from the cities, it would be among the rusty settlements of an old-settled country, . . . in the towns about Boston . . . and not in the backwoods of Maine.[36]

He admired the logger as a rugged individualist who lived in nature, not among the more "respectable" segments of society. Even though later in *The Maine Woods* Thoreau denounces logging—he was turned off by the loggers' role in the marketing of nature—he idealized the ways in which loggers lived the "sort of border life" that Thoreau aimed for himself.[37]

We can find a number of parallels between Thoreau's inquiry and that of the sociologist. The discipline of sociology grew out of suspicion of authority figures and as a means of understanding new social problems and class issues that emerged during the industrial revolution. It has grown into a field that is important for its comparative analysis of values and cultures. The public sociologist has evolved into an intellectual who is concerned with viewing social reality from all perspectives and unmasking the many layers of society. Whether exploring different social class levels or deconstructing the accepted goals of society, these efforts originate from a consciousness that holds sacred particular values and objectives. As a writer and social critic, Thoreau's intentions and approaches are steeped in this same type of consciousness and inquiry. He looked beyond the obvious. He questioned power structures and the commonly accepted goals of society. He explored the relativity of ideas and meaning systems, and even employed qualitative methods to do so. While he certainly was not a sociologist in the modern sense, his work suggests he was closer to social science inquiry than the traditional labels of "essayist" and "poet" suggest.

Notes

1. Henry David Thoreau, "Walden," in *The Portable Thoreau*, rev. ed., ed. Carl Bode (New York: Penguin, 1987), 363.

2. Lewis Hyde, "Introduction: Prophetic Excursions," in *The Essays of Henry David Thoreau*, ed. Lewis Hyde (New York: North Point Press, 2002), xxi.

3. Hyde, "Introduction: Prophetic Excursions," xxi–xxiv.

4. Henry David Thoreau, *The Journal of Henry David Thoreau*, ed. Bradford Torrey and Francis Allen (Boston: Houghton Mifflin, 1906), VIII: 44.

5. Thoreau, "Walden," 266.

6. Thoreau, "Walden," 363.

7. Thoreau, "Walden," 385–86.

8. See Hyde's "Introduction: Prophetic Excursions" for additional discussion of Thoreau's interest in awakening the reader.

9. Thoreau, "Walden," 343.

10. Thoreau, "Walden," 349.

11. Thoreau, Walden," 348–49 (italics mine).

12. Peter Berger, *An Invitation to Sociology: A Humanistic Perspective* (New York: Bantam/Doubleday, 1963), 38 (italics mine).

13. Berger, *An Invitation to Sociology*, 62.

14. Thoreau, "Walden," 362.

15. Henry David Thoreau, "Life without Principle," in *The Portable Thoreau*, rev ed , ed. Carl Bode (New York: Penguin, 1987), 650.

16. Robert Sayre, *Thoreau and the American Indians* (Princeton, NJ: Princeton University Press, 1977), 123.

17. In his article "The 'Domestic Air' of Wilderness: Henry Thoreau and Joe Polis in the Maine Woods," *Weber Studies* 14, no. 3 (Fall 1997): 38–48, Tom Lynch points out that Thoreau's guide, Joe Polis, was an expert in Penobscot culture, a shaman, and even served as a representative of his tribe in Washington, DC. Polis, though, lived in a two-story house and was "literate" in white culture. He was, as Lynch states, able to "straddle" the divide between the white and Penobscot cultures.

18. Robert Richardson Jr., *Henry Thoreau: A Life of the Mind* (Berkeley and Los Angeles: University of California Press, 1986), 301.

19. Richardson, *Henry Thoreau*, 282.

20. Richardson, *Henry Thoreau*, 282.

21. Richardson, *Henry Thoreau*, 223.

22. Lawrence Buell, *The Environmental Imagination: Thoreau, Nature Writing and the Foundation of American Culture* (Cambridge, MA: Belknap Press of Harvard University Press, 1995), 211.

23. Buell, *The Environmental Imagination*, 211.

24. Sayre, *Thoreau and the American Indians*, xiv.

25. Sayre, *Thoreau and the American Indians*, 213.

26. Richardson, *Henry Thoreau*, 206.

27. Richardson, *Henry Thoreau*, 81.

28. Thoreau, "Walden," 383.

29. I have pulled on the ideas of Peter Berger's (1963) "unrespectability" motif, from *An Introduction to Sociology*, to explore this aspect of Thoreau's work. Those possessing this characteristic look to all segments of society when examining social life, or, in Berger's words, look at social life "not only from the perspective of the city hall, but also from that of city jail" (47).

30. Thoreau, "Walden," 400.

31. Henry David Thoreau, "Civil Disobedience," in *The Portable Thoreau*, rev. ed., ed. Carl Bode (New York: Penguin, 1987), 127–30.

32. Henry David Thoreau, *The Maine Woods*, ed. Joseph Moldenhauer (Princeton, NJ: Princeton University Press, 1972), 19–20.

33. Thoreau, *The Maine Woods*, 34

34. Thoreau, *The Maine Woods*, 42–43.

35. Thoreau, *The Maine Woods*, 47–48.

36. Thoreau, *The Maine Woods*, 22–23.

37. Henry David Thoreau, "Walking," in *The Portable Thoreau*, rev. ed., ed. Carl Bode (New York: Penguin, 1987), 625.

CHAPTER SIX

~

Thoreau as a Model for "Reimagining" Sociology

During his lifetime Thoreau challenged those around him. Emerson was quick to make this point in the eulogy at his good friend's funeral. However, Thoreau continues to challenge those who read his works. For generations he has confronted readers with the task of self-examination as well as the act of scrutinizing the way we live our lives and what we live for. His works also present the dilemma we addressed in chapter 1: how to classify him. Is he a poet, essayist, and all-around literary icon? Is he an activist, environmentalist, or naturalist? Should he be remembered and looked to as a political philosopher? Can he be all of these at once? For many, he remains in only one of these classifications because they have chosen to impose their own categories on him, an act Thoreau himself might scoff at with aggravation. However, if we approach Thoreau's work the way he approached nature and life itself, we find that a one-dimensional view of Thoreau is an injustice: There is always something new and different to discover. That is the truth by which Thoreau lived and that has been the point of this work.

For those who have come to this manuscript from outside of the discipline of sociology I hope to have provided you with new ways to "see" Thoreau and his work. He certainly shares some common soil with the roots of sociology. Though he was a steadfast individual until his death, he was shaped by and reacted to the social context in which he found himself—rapid economic, political, and technological changes. Thoreau's intellectual lineage can be traced to early thinkers in the development of sociological theory, including Jean-Jacques Rousseau, Immanuel Kant, and Adam Smith. More importantly, though, Thoreau had a more sophisticated approach to looking at society than many have given the "crank poet" credit for. He did not simply stand on a soapbox and preach or rant in disgust. There was a framework, as well as clear methods and objectives, behind his work. Beyond simply introducing readers to the wonders of nature, he unveiled the jungle of society by peeling back its many layers of complexity. He explored how social structures, such as the economic and political systems, shaped individuals in a particular cultural context. He questioned power structures and the commonly accepted goals of society. He also made efforts to deconstruct relative definitions of civilization, savage, development, and poverty; yet, contrary to popular opinion, Thoreau was not antiprogress. In fact, he employed cutting-edge systematic methods to examine natural and social phenomena, from the unnoticed pond to the invisible pauper. He had an in-depth understanding of science, but he often preferred a more qualitative approach to inquiry. Beyond Emerson or Tocqueville, Thoreau's topics span a broad range of social issues and societies. His canvas had no disciplinary or cultural boundaries. While he was not a sociologist, there was a lot of sociology within his work. An appreciation for this side of Thoreau can bring new insights when reading or rereading his works.

Beyond the individual reader, though, Thoreau offers new opportunities for disciplinary self-reflection and critique to a range of academic fields. In the remainder of this chapter, however, I will focus specifically on how sociology can benefit from his work. I began in chapter 1 by exploring and critiquing the dogmatic approach sociology has taken toward its canon and the inclusion of theorists in discussion and curriculum. This is where we find the first challenge Thoreau can provide to sociology—a reexamination of which individuals are included in discussions about social theory. Though the discipline uses nonsociologists as "founders" of sociological thought, few efforts are currently made to look at nonsociologists of the past and present to consider what contributions they might make to the discipline. As it has become a legitimate and bona fide academic discipline, sociology has become an exclusive realm of knowledge that only "trained" sociologists can conduct. Sociology's claim as the "queen of all sciences" demonstrates the discipline's own sense of self-importance in relation to other academic fields. In fact, some might view going back at this point in time to examine thinkers outside the discipline to be counterproductive, or a move backward, because this would require an acknowledgement that we need to draw on other disciplines outside of sociology. That argument is partially correct. Sociology does need to draw on other disciplines, but such a move is a step forward. After all, most sociologists view the deconstruction of boundaries and definitions that are created and imposed by humans as progress. Why shouldn't sociology itself be fair game for such scrutiny? Why shouldn't our canonical criteria be deconstructed and our course reading lists reexamined? Other authors have made compelling arguments for sociology to examine its own rigid self-construction or face intellectual stagnation and staleness.[1] I have tried to contribute to their campaign by providing evidence that links a more "literary" figure, Thoreau, to sociological consciousness and inquiry. *While there is no argument here for including Thoreau in the canon*, I do make the case that Thoreau, and others like him, can make a legitimate contribution to sociological theory and that thinkers like him could infuse new theoretical direction and ideas into sociological discussion.

Toward a "Fruitful" Dialogue: Comparing Thoreau to Others

Thoreau had a unique insider's view of the United States at a time when the social and physical landscape was rapidly changing. He was a theorist who uniquely linked positivism and Romanticism. From his ideas on the state of nature to his observations on the individual in American society and the effects of modernity, there are immediate connections and comparisons to be made between Thoreau's work and the work of other thinkers already used within sociology. For example, Thoreau's insider account of America differed from the observations of Alexis de Tocqueville and Harriet Martineau. Which account was the most accurate and what could be learned from a comparison? There are parallels to and contrasts with other theorists as well. Charles Montesquieu, Gaetano Mosca, Vilfredo Pareto, and Antonio Gramsci all explored the relationship between the individual and the collective good. How do Thoreau's views on the individual and society differ from these theorists? How would Thoreau's views on modernity and rationalization compare to later thinkers? Georg Simmel's ideas about self-actualization and autonomy and Thorsten Veblen's conspicuous consumption certainly have parallels to Thoreau's work. Potential connections to specific areas of sociology could also be explored in further detail. For example, what contributions can Thoreau's ideas on progress, including his comparison of the "savage" with the "civilized," make to current sociological theories of development? How might environmental sociologists draw on his work? Making these connections to other theorists and specialized areas within sociology would certainly allow us to better determine where Thoreau stands in the evolution of social thought. It would also expand the possibilities of sociology by infusing theoretical discussions with an innovative and novel perspective.

Sociology as a Technical Act

One area of sociology that could certainly use this novel perspective is the discipline's dominant research paradigm—an unbending approach to inquiry fixated on understanding society in mechanical ways. In chapter 1 I briefly discussed the potentially damaging trend of what C. Wright Mills termed "abstracted empiricism," an approach to social inquiry that he argues has "seized upon one juncture in the process of work" and allowed it to "dominate the mind."[2] Mills, Berger, and a range of other sociologists have commented on the tendency of sociological inquiry to be increasingly conducted as a dry, technical act in which method is cultivated for its own sake, and the sociologist evolves into nothing more than a bureaucratic statistician. Mills even believed that this trend would inhibit the possibilities of sociology by limiting the selection and formation of research problems to certain topics; as he states, it is our methodology itself that often determines the "problems."[3] Indeed, empiricism often has a habit of ensuring that some things get noticed—those that are measurable within the structure of quantitative research—while others do not. This can be seen in the contemporary criteria used to determine which sociological research projects get funded, decisions that often depend not on what is most important or interesting, but on what the *bureaucratic sources* have defined as important. Just as Thoreau argued before him, Mills believed that our "training often incapacitates us" by imposing fixed categories, such as language and methods, on social phenomena.[4]

The belief that the practice of sociology is "real" only if it has been run through "the mill of the Statistic Ritual"[5] results in a number of problems for sociology. To Mills, the alignment of sociologists with administrative structure and bureaucratic interests has shifted our focus away from the public realm and suppressed the individual sociologist's imagination in the process.[6] Peter Berger is even more forceful in his description of the implications: "As a result, they have found nothing of significance about any aspect of social life, since in science as in love a concentration on technique is quite likely to lead to *impotence*."[7] Not only does this approach create a very limited view of social life, it also creates an undemocratic approach to gathering and disseminating knowledge. It severely decreases the accessibility of sociology to the average citizen. For example, in their preoccupation with technical skills, sociologists have become less competent in their use of language, which diminishes the common ground and means of communication with the broader public.[8] As sociological inquiry becomes the exclusive realm of "trained quantitative sociologists," the potential of sociology to reach average citizens literally becomes stifled in a coded language of statistics and data that only the technician can understand. As sociologists, we need to reflect on whether we are writing to reach only other social scientists or if we seek a broader public audience. If we seek to disseminate public knowledge, we must find more accessible and democratic means of communication. This will require that we look outside of our traditional methods in search of an alternative to social inquiry as merely a technical act.

Thoreau as Craftsman of Inquiry

What does any of this have to do with an eighteenth-century "literary" figure such as Thoreau? If we want to heed Thoreau's warning about the limitations of science and Mills's cautions about a strictly quantitative sociology, we would be wise to approach social inquiry more as a craft than a technical or mechanical act.[9] Mills in particular proposed that sociologists should work to develop their "craft" by keeping a journal. This would not only build a habit of writing, but would also develop powers of expression and self-reflective habits to keep a connection to one's inner world. The ability to take good notes and to write would help sociologists to "translate our experiences," giving them form.[10] Mills even referred to such journaling or note taking as a "curious sort of 'literary' journal"—a habit he saw as imperative to intellectual production. Indeed, he argued that much of the writing in the social sciences has no voice—it is impersonal "prose manufactured by a machine."[11] Yet in *The Sociological Imagination*, Mills highlights the need for an opposite approach—a "release of imagination" and a "playfulness of mind" that would separate the true sociologist from the research technician:[12]

> The idea is to use a variety of viewpoints: . . . ask yourself how would a political scientist . . . approach this, . . . experimental psychologist, or this historian? You try to think in terms of a variety of viewpoints and in this way let your mind become a moving prism catching light from as many angles as possible. . . .
> Always keep your eyes open to the image of man—the generic notion of his human nature—which by your work you are assuming and implying. . . . Keep your eyes open to the varieties of individuality. . . . Use what you see and what you imagine, as the clues to your study of the human variety.[13]

Berger made a similar case by arguing that sociologists needed to focus more on the commonplace, perfect the art of listening, and look to other disciplines, including the humanities. Sociology, he argued, is hardly the "last word on human life."[14] The title *An Invitation to Sociology: A Humanistic Perspective* hints at one of the most important arguments of his book—that sociology needs a more humanistic approach and more ongoing communication with other disciplines if it wants to understand the human condition:

> In addition to these human values that are inherent in the scientific enterprise of sociology itself, the discipline has other traits that assign it to the immediate vicinity of the humanities, if they do not, indeed, indicate that it belongs fully with them. . . . [S]ociology is vitally concerned with what is, after all, the principal subject matter of the humanities—the human condition itself. . . .
>
> Such an understanding of the humanistic place of sociology implies an openness of mind and a catholicity of vision. . . .
>
> Openness to the humanistic scope of sociology further implies an ongoing communication with other disciplines that are vitally concerned with exploring the human condition.[15]

This final point underlines the entire purpose of my work herein. Thinkers like Thoreau, who come to us through the humanities, offer lessons on what a more catholic approach to sociology would look like in practice.

Whether he was exploring the social landscape of loggers, surveying land, or charting seed dispersal, Thoreau conceived of his inquiry as a craft. Far from simply relying on the technical methods of science, Thoreau aimed to find a middle ground between the objective and subjective views by putting imagination and wonder back into inquiry and by taking a more integrative approach. Some argue that he was the last major American writer to believe he could be simultaneously a scientist and a "man of letters" on the same project.[16] It is important to recognize how the techniques of the "literary" craft, including his daily habits, aided Thoreau in his endeavors to understand the world around him. To begin, he spent hours each day observing his surroundings to develop ideas, and then recorded these observations and reflections in his journals. His entries also included scientific recordings, poetry, and reflections on what he was reading. He used journaling as a way to sort and analyze his thoughts and to further develop his powers of expression. To Thoreau, writing was an integral part of his discovery process. Self-reflection and writing were important to him for understanding what was going on around him and how he related to it. He spent hours each day honing his ability to express his ideas in written form. Thoreau was able to move beyond the empirical viewpoint and give form in his writing to phenomena because of his more "literary" or artistic approach toward perspective and his emphasis on wakefulness and seeing.

It was Thoreau's fascination with sensory experience and "sauntering" that helped him to master perspective. As an observer, he was interested in the "schooling of the eye and hand,"[17] which was based in sensory experience and the language of the senses.[18] He relied heavily on sight and sound; some of his most exquisite passages include descriptions of visual and aural phenomena. Wary of the narrowness of simply scientific measures, Thoreau often employed sauntering as a way of observing. This form of local travel, which involved walking and recording impressions from his observations, brought a different and more organic way of seeing.[19] Thoreau described it as "walking so gently as to hear the finest sounds—the faculties being in repose—your mind must not perspire."[20] To truly saunter, he believed, an individual must be able to abandon social goals and expectations. Sauntering became a self-reflective way Thoreau could examine phenomena and his refine his capabilities as an observer.[21] It involved observing intently and the art of listening. We need only read a sample of Thoreau's work to realize how important sauntering and the sensory experience were to his work:

> This is a delicious evening, when the whole body is one sense, and imbibes delight through every pore. I go and come with a strange liberty in Nature, a part of herself. As I walk along the stony shore of the pond in my shirt sleeves, though it is cool as well as cloudy and windy, and I see nothing special to attract me, all the elements are unusually congenial to me. The bullfrogs trump to usher in the night and the note of the whippoorwill is borne on the rippling wind from over the water. Sympathy with the fluttering alder and poplar leaves almost takes away my breath; yet like the lake, my serenity is rippled, not ruffled.[22]

Thoreau mastered the artist's more qualitative skills of listening, observing, and articulating these realities in a manner that reached and connected with a grand audience. This more "literary" approach to the craft of inquiry—perspective, writing, wonder, the art of listening quietly, and interdisciplinary study—was not only integral to Thoreau's attempt to understand the human condition, it certainly includes skills for sociologists to emulate in their attempt to understand and represent society.

The Art of Sociological Inquiry

Ultimately, the sociologist and the artist are often left with the same challenge—to observe the realities of society and, using the tools of the trade, to articulate them. And while the tools may seem worlds apart—the sociologist employs data and diagrams, while the artist uses paint or clay—is the sociological perspective that different from the artistic perspective? There can be no doubt that artists have been some of the most accurate observers of social life. Certainly, many artists have succeeded in speaking to the human condition and impacting the everyday life of individuals. They have even been catalysts of social movement and social change. Sociologists would be fortunate to have such an audience and social influence. Yet it is prudent to consider the parallels between the artist and the sociologist. One of the artist's most important strengths is the ability to *take the role and perspective of the other*, a task we ask of all students when attempting to teach the concept of the sociological imagination. Just as there is no sociology without considering multiple views, there is no art without perspective. Indeed, some of our most celebrated artists have mastered the skill of shifting perspectives. They are also capable of *turning our attention to what is typically unseen*. No subject is too mundane, small, or insignificant. They teach us that there is wonder in all, offering a view of the commonplace and the ugly as well as the beautiful. Through their chosen subjects, artists argue that the ordinary deserves acknowledgement and consideration. Furthermore, when the artist is at work, she is often as systematic as the mathematician—crafting words, observing minute details, and laboring to reproduce an image, describe or portray a situation. With wonder, awe, and amazement, the artist picks up on the detailed lines on a laborer's face or the patterns of a flower. Such efforts take skill, discipline, and time—characteristics we do not commonly associate with "artistic types." Finally, the artist often *looks at the world as an outsider*. This is a perspective that allows her to stand apart and look both objectively and subjectively, often simultaneously. This also provides a sense of freedom to the artist as an observer of the world. The artist rarely looks for inspiration from the bureaucratic funding world. Few artists choose their topics from a "call for papers" or "request for proposals." Unlike many within the social sciences, her muse is not tied to the structure of authority.

Conclusion

Thoreau's success in portraying the human condition and reaching individuals around the world—including founders of major global social movements—lies in his use of these more "artistic" capabilities and methods. He drew on his "artist's eye" to capture the mundane, to unveil social norms, and to speak to the human condition. He also used the craft of writing to articulate these ideas in a cogent and everlasting manner that has provided meaning to generations. However, he uniquely combined this approach with a humanistic sociological consciousness. He approached natural and social inquiry as a craft, not a sterile science. His true mission was to "front the essential facts of life," and to provide a true account of life, "real or sublime."[23] So why is Thoreau, or any other "literary" social critic, worth examining from a sociological perspective? Such figures challenge us to rethink the boundaries of the discipline, the criteria we use for these boundaries, and the weight we attribute to different methods of social inquiry. Thoreau's work in particular speaks to the human condition and raises many sociological questions without remaining simply a technical body of work. His writings address many of the same issues raised by important figures within sociology, such as Karl Marx and Jean-Jacques Rousseau. Awaiting our analysis is a range of theoretical comparisons and applications of Thoreau's work that could provide new and interesting directions for social theory.

However, Thoreau also provides sociology with a model for resisting a strict empirical approach to social inquiry through his use of a more integrative and interdisciplinary approach to inquiry. He was at once a natural historian, a well-trained measurer of natural phenomena, a quasi anthropologist, a social philosopher and analyst, and a writer with a more literary style. There is no doubt that his expertise in all of these disciplines provided him with a more well-rounded and valid perception of reality. In other words, Thoreau's example seems to prove that an epistemology of specialization, whether through one particular discipline or a particular research method, is an incomplete way of viewing the social world. For sociology, figures like Thoreau should reinforce the need for interdisciplinary inquiry. His focus on integrating science with a more "literary" or artistic way of seeing the world corresponds to the calls by important theorists like Mills and Berger for more humanistic methods in sociology. Sociology can learn from Thoreau's "genius" for perspective, particularly his focus on sensory perception and his "playfulness of mind," as Mills called it. Thoreau's view of inquiry as a craft provides sociology with a number of lessons that will encourage sociologists to think further about writing, expression, reflection, and perspective as part of the "craft" of sociology. *All of these characteristics will promote resistance to abstracted empiricism.*

As the landscape of consumer culture becomes more ubiquitous, Thoreau's emphasis on individual "awakening" remains relevant, and even vital, to an authentic existence in twenty-first-century society. Yet Thoreau's work also serves as an important reminder that for sociologists, the redemptive power of our discipline depends on our abilities to reach and connect with a broader audience. Social critics like Thoreau have not only demonstrated the ability to paint an authentic portrait of society, they have succeeded where many sociologists have not in awakening and mobilizing countless citizens to reexamine their own worlds. By speaking to the human condition in a poignant and meaningful way, Thoreau's ideas have reached a large audience and, in the process, have helped bring global social justice to humanity and nature. Beyond just personal inspiration, Thoreau's work can help us to reexamine the extent to which "imagination" is really a part of sociology. Can we "imagine" what a more interdisciplinary sociology—a discipline that takes note of calls by C. Wright Mills and Peter Berger for sociology to align itself closer to the humanities in order to better understand the human condition—might yield in application? Can we possibly "imagine" a time when mainstream sociology might reflect Thoreau's perspective on knowledge and inquiry by leaving behind the "harnesses" it has created?

> What we call knowledge is often our positive ignorance; ignorance our negative knowledge. By long years of patient industry and reading of the newspapers,—for what are the libraries of science but files of newspapers?—a man accumulates a myriad facts, lays them up in his memory, and then when in some spring of his life he saunters abroad into the great Fields of thought, he as it were goes to grass like a horse, and leaves all his harness behind in the stable.[24]

To those who cling to a traditionalist and insular approach to sociology, the question I have just posed may seem mundane, irrelevant, and even irreverent. Yet many thought the same of the hermit who built his cabin beside a pond.

Notes

1. See George Ritzer and Douglas Goodman, "Introduction: Toward a More Open Canon," in *The Blackwell Companion to Major Social Theorists*, ed. George Ritzer and Douglas Goodman (Malden, MA: Blackwell, 2002), 1–21; and Patricia Lengermann and Jill Niebrugge-Brantley, *The Women Founders: Sociological and Social Theory 1830–1930* (Boston: McGraw-Hill, 1998).

2. C. Wright Mills, *The Sociological Imagination* (New York: Oxford University Press, 1959), 50.

3. Mills, *The Sociological Imagination*, 50–75.

4. Mills, *The Sociological Imagination*, 212.

5. Mills, *The Sociological Imagination*, 71.

6. Mills, *The Sociological Imagination*, 102, 105–6, 177–94.

7. Peter Berger, *An Invitation to Sociology: A Humanistic Perspective* (New York: Bantam/Doubleday, 1963), 13.

8. In *An Invitation to Sociology*, 12, Berger chides sociology for its insensitivity to the use of language.

9. Mills, *The Sociological Imagination*, 195–226.

10. Mills, *The Sociological Imagination*, 199.

11. Mills, *The Sociological Imagination*, 221.

12. Mills, *The Sociological Imagination*, 211, 215.

13. Mills, *The Sociological Imagination*, 214, 225.

14. Berger, *An Invitation to Sociology*, 164.

15. Berger, *An Invitation to Sociology*, 167–68.

16. This argument is made by Laura Dassow Walls in *Seeing New Worlds: Henry David Thoreau and Nineteenth-Century Natural Science* (Madison: University of Wisconsin Press, 1995) and by John Hildebidle in *Thoreau: A Naturalist's Liberty* (Cambridge, MA: Harvard University Press, 1983).

17. Henry David Thoreau, "Autumnal Tints," in *The Natural History Essays*, ed. Robert Sattelmeyer (Salt Lake City, UT: Peregrine Smith, 1980), 287.

18. For a more in-depth discussion on Thoreau's use of sensory perception see Kerry McSweeney, *The Language of the Senses: Sensory-Perceptual Dynamics in Wordsworth, Coleridge, Thoreau, Whitman, and Dickinson* (Montreal: McGill-Queen's University Press, 1998).

19. Peter Blakemore, "Reading Home: Thoreau, Literature and the Phenomena of Inhabitation," in *Thoreau's Sense of Place: Essays in American Environmental Writing*, ed. Richard Schneider (Iowa City: University of Iowa Press, 2000), 115.

20. Henry David Thoreau, *Journal*, eds. Bradford Torrey and Francis Allen (Boston: Houghton Mifflin and Company, 1906), III: 329.

21. David Robinson, "The Written World: Place and History in Thoreau's 'A Walk to Wachusett,'" in *Thoreau's Sense of Place: Essays in American Environmental Writing*, ed. Richard Schneider (Iowa City: University of Iowa Press, 2000), 83.

22. Henry David Thoreau, "Walden," in *The Portable Thoreau*, rev. ed., ed. Carl Bode (New York: Penguin, 1987), 380.

23. Thoreau, "Walden," 363.

24. Henry David Thoreau, "Walking," in *The Portable Thoreau*, rev. ed., ed. Carl Bode (New York: Penguin, 1987), 622–23.

~

Bibliography

Abbot, Phillip. "Henry David Thoreau, the State of Nature, and the Redemption of Liberalism." *Journal of Politics* 47 (1985): 183–208.

Anderson, Charles. *The Magic Circle of Walden*. New York: Holt, Rinehart and Wilson, 1968.

Bakratcheva, Albena. "Henry David Thoreau and the Spiritual Emancipation in Bulgaria." Paper presented at the Annual Thoreau Society Meeting, Concord, MA, 1993. LiterNet.revolta.com/publish/alba/texts/_fulb-st.htm (accessed May 10, 2002).

Baym, Nancy. "Thoreau's View of Science." *Journal of the History of Ideas* 26 (1965): 221–34.

Beck, Sanderson. *The Way to Peace: The Great Peacemakers, Philosophy of Peace, and Efforts Toward World Peace*. New York: Mind and Miracle Press, 1986.

Berger, Peter. *An Invitation to Sociology: A Humanistic Perspective*. New York: Bantam/Doubleday, 1963.

Berger, Peter, and Thomas Luckman. *The Social Construction of Reality: A Treatise in the Sociology of Knowledge*. Garden City, NY: Anchor Books, 1967.

Bernard, L. L., and Jessie Bernard. *The Origins of American Sociology: The Social Science Movement in the United States*. New York: Russell and Russell, 1965.

Blakemore, Peter. "Reading Home: Thoreau, Literature and the Phenomena of Inhabitation." In *Thoreau's Sense of Place: Essays in American Environmental Writing*, edited by Richard Schneider, 115–32. Iowa City: University of Iowa Press, 2000.

Bode, Carl. "Introduction." In *The Portable Thoreau*, rev. ed., edited by Carl Bode, 1–27. New York: Penguin, 1987.

Bodily, Christopher. "Henry David Thoreau: The Instrumental Transcendentalist?" *Journal of Economic Issues* 21, no. 1 (1987): 203–18.

Botkin, Daniel. *No Man's Garden: Thoreau and a New Vision for Civilization and Nature*. Washington, DC: Island Press, 2001.

Buell, Lawrence. *The Environmental Imagination: Thoreau, Nature Writing and the Formation of American Culture*. Cambridge, MA: Belknap Press of Harvard University Press, 1995.

———. *New England Literary Culture*. Cambridge: Cambridge University Press, 1986.

———. "Thoreau and the Natural Environment." In *The Cambridge Companion to Henry David Thoreau*, edited by Joel Myerson, 171–93. New York: Cambridge University Press, 1995.

Cain, William. "Henry David Thoreau 1817–1862: A Brief Biography." In *A Historical Guide to Henry David Thoreau*, edited by William Cain, 11–57. New York: Oxford University Press, 2000.

Chadha, Yogesh. *Gandhi: A Life*. New York: John Wiley and Sons, 1999.

Coser, Lewis A. *Masters of Sociological Thought: Ideas in Historical and Social Context*. 2nd ed. Fort Worth, TX: Harcourt Brace Jovanovich, 1977.

Darwin, Charles. *The Origin of Species*. New York: Signet Classics, 2003.

Diggins, John. "Thoreau, Marx and the Riddle of Alienation." *Social Research* 39, no. 4 (1972): 571–98.

Duncan, David James. "Foreword." In *Thoreau on Water: Reflecting Heaven*, edited by Laura Walls and J. Parker Huber, ix–xiv. Boston: Mariner, 2001.

Editors of the Seven Arts. "Henry David Thoreau (1817–1917)." In *Thoreau: A Collection of Critical Essays*, edited by Sherman Paul, 9–12. Englewood Cliffs, NJ: Prentice-Hall, 1962.

France, Robert Lawrence. "Introduction." In *Thoreau on Water: Reflecting Heaven*, edited by Robert France, xix–xxi. Boston: Mariner, 2001.

Frederick, Michael. "Transcendental Ethos: A Study of Thoreau's Social Philosophy and its Consistency in Relation to Antebellum Reform." MA thesis, Harvard University, 1998. thoreau.eserver.org/MJF/MJF.html (accessed May 12, 2002).

Friesen, Victor. "Seeing Beyond the Verge of Sight: Thoreau's Nature as Incessant Miracle." Paper presented at the Symposium on Science, Spirituality, and the Environment, St. Catharines, ON, 1999.

Gandhi, Mohandas. "Hind Swaraj or Indian Home Rule." *Indian Opinion*, December 11 and 18, 1909.

———. *Non-violent Resistance*. Edited by Bharatan Kumarappa. New York: Schocken Books, 1961.

Gilmore, Michael. *American Romanticism and the Marketplace*. Chicago: University of Chicago Press, 1985.

Glendon, M. A. "Rousseau and the Revolt against Reason." *First Things* 96 (October 1999): 42–47.

Glick, Wendell. "Henry David Thoreau (1817–1862)." In *The Heath Anthology of American Literature*, 3rd ed., edited by P. Lauter, 1964–2062. Lexington, MA: D. C. Heath, 1990.

Gougeon, Leonard. "Thoreau and Reform." In *The Cambridge Companion to Henry David Thoreau*, edited by Joel Myerson, 191–214. New York: Cambridge University Press, 1995.

Guthrie, James. *Above Time: Emerson's and Thoreau's Temporal Revolutions*. Columbia: University of Missouri Press, 2001.

Hampson, Thomas. "The American Renaissance & Transcendentalism." In *I Hear America Singing*. 1997. www.pbs.org/wnet/ihas/icon/transcend.html (accessed May 14, 2002).

———. "Romanticism." In *I Hear America Singing*. 1997. www.pbs.org/wnet/ihas/icon/romanticism.html (accessed May 14, 2002).

Harding, Walter. *The Days of Henry David Thoreau: A Biography*. Princeton, NJ: Princeton University Press, 1992.

———. "Thoreau's Reputation." In *The Cambridge Companion to Henry David Thoreau*, edited by Joel Myerson, 1–11. New York: Cambridge University Press.

———. *Variorum Civil Disobedience*. New York: Irvington Publications, 1968.

Harding, Walter, and Michael Meyer. *The New Thoreau Handbook*. New York: New York University Press, 1980.

Hawthorn, Geoffrey. "No Context, No History: The Sociological Canon." In *Canon vs. Culture: Reflections on the Current Debate*, edited by Jan Gorak, 43–54. New York: Garland, 2001.

Hildebidle, John. *Thoreau: A Naturalist's Liberty*. Cambridge, MA: Harvard University Press, 1983.

Hyde, Lewis. "Introduction: Prophetic Excursions." In *The Essays of Henry David Thoreau*, edited by L. Hyde, vii–li. New York: North Point Press, 2002.

Jones, S. A. *Pertaining to Thoreau*. Folcroft, PA: Folcroft Press, 1969.

Kant, Immanuel. *Critique of Pure Reason*. Edited by Paul Guyer and Allen Wood. New York: Cambridge University Press, 1999.

Kasser, Tim. *The High Price of Materialism*. Cambridge, MA: MIT Press, 2003.

Kessel, David. "Fromm, Mills, Berger and Sociology." The Sociology Shop. 2002. www.angelfire.com/or/sociologyshop/fromills.html (accessed May 12, 2002).

King, Martin Luther, Jr. *The Autobiography of Martin Luther King, Jr.* Edited by Clayborne Carson. New York: Time Warner, 1998.

Layard, Richard. *Happiness: Lessons from a New Science*. New York: Penguin, 2005.

Lemert, Charles. *Sociology after the Crisis*. Boulder, CO: Westview, 1995.

Lenat, Richard. "A Brief Introduction to the Works of Henry David Thoreau." The Thoreau Reader. 2001. eserver.org/thoreau/brief.html (accessed June 6, 2002).

Lengermann, Patricia, and Jill Niebrugge-Brantley. *The Women Founders: Sociology and Social Theory, 1830–1930*. Boston: McGraw-Hill, 1998.

Lerner, Max. "Thoreau: No Hermit." In *Thoreau: A Collection of Critical Essays*, edited by Sherman Paul, 122–54. Englewood Cliffs, NJ: Prentice-Hall, 1962.

Levine, Robert. *A Geography of Time*. New York: Basic Books, 1998.

Lynch, Tom. "The 'Domestic Air' of Wilderness: Henry Thoreau and Joe Polis in the Maine Woods." *Weber Studies* 14, no. 3 (Fall 1997): 38–48.

McGrath, James. "Ten Ways of Seeing Landscape in Walden and Beyond." In *Thoreau's Sense of Place: Essays in American Environmental Writing*, edited by Richard Schneider, 149–64. Iowa City: University of Iowa Press, 2000.

McGuire, Patrick. "A Carrier Pigeon to Phoenix: The Chrysalis of Sociology." In *Towards a Second Dimension: A Sociology Reader*, edited by Patrick McGuire and Linda Pertusati, 124–45. Dubuque, IA: Kendall/Hunt, 1998.

McIntosh, James. *Thoreau as Romantic Naturalist: His Shifting Stance toward Nature*. Ithaca, NY: Cornell University Press, 1974.

McSweeney, Kerry. *The Language of the Senses: Sensory Perception Dynamics in Wordsworth, Coleridge, Thoreau, Whitman, and Dickinson*. Montreal: McGill-Queen's University Press, 1998.

Mills, C. Wright. "The Promise." In *The Sociological Imagination*, 3–24. New York: Oxford University Press, 1959.

———. *The Sociological Imagination*. New York: Oxford University Press, 1959.

Moller, Mary Elkins. *Thoreau in the Human Community*. Amherst: University of Massachusetts Press, 1980.

Neufeldt, Leonard. *The Economist: Henry Thoreau and Enterprise*. New York: Oxford University Press, 1989.

Newman, Lance. "Thoreau's Natural Community and Utopian Socialism." *American Literature* 75, no. 3 (2003): 516–44.

Oelschlaeger, Max. *The Idea of Wilderness: From Prehistory to the Age of Ecology*. New Haven, CT: Yale University Press, 1991.

Paul, Sherman. "Introduction." In *Thoreau: A Collection of Critical Essays*, 1–7. Englewood Cliffs, NJ: Prentice-Hall, 1962.

Peck, H. Daniel. *Thoreau's Morning Work: Memory and Perception in "A Week on the Concord and Merrimack Rivers," "The Journal," and "Walden."* New Haven, CT: Yale University Press, 1990.

Porte, Joel. *Emerson and Thoreau: The Contemporary Reviews*. New York: Cambridge University Press, 1992.

———. *Emerson and Thoreau: Transcendentalists in Conflict*. Middletown, CT: Wesleyan University Press, 1966.

Quetchenbach, Bernard. "Sauntering in the Industrial Wilderness." In *Thoreau's Sense of Place: Essays in American Environmental Writing*, edited by Richard Schneider, 165–78. Iowa City: University of Iowa Press, 2000.

Rice, John. "Romantic Modernism and the Self." *Hedgehog Review* 1 (Fall 1999). www.virginia.edu/iasc/hh/THRtoc1–1.html (accessed May 2, 2002).

Richardson, Robert, Jr. *Henry Thoreau: A Life of the Mind*. Berkeley and Los Angeles: University of California Press, 1986.

———. "Thoreau and Science." In *American Literature and Science*, edited by Robert Scholnik, 110–27. Lexington: University Press of Kentucky, 1992.

Ritzer, George. *Classical Sociological Theory*. 3rd ed. Boston: McGraw-Hill, 2000.

———. "Herbert Spencer." In *Classical Sociological Theory*, 3rd ed., 113–46. Boston: McGraw-Hill, 2000.

———. *Modern Sociological Theory*. Boston: McGraw-Hill, 2000.

Ritzer, George, and Douglas Goodman. "Introduction: Toward a More Open Canon." In *The Blackwell Companion to Major Social Theorists*, edited by George Ritzer and Douglas Goodman, 1–21. Malden, MA: Blackwell, 2002.

Robinson, David. "The Written World: Place and History in Thoreau's 'A Walk to Wachusett.'" In *Thoreau's Sense of Place: Essays in American Environmental Writing*, edited by Richard Schneider, 83–92. Iowa City: University of Iowa Press, 2000.

Rosenthal, Steven. "An Egalitarian Course in Classical Sociological Theory." The Etext Archives. 1995. www.etext.org/Politics/Progressive.Sociologists/marthas-corner/ Rosenthal:Egalitarian_Course_in_Classical_Sociology (accessed July 10, 2002).

Rosenwald, Lawrence. "The Theory, Practice and Influence of Thoreau's 'Civil Disobedience.'" In *A Historical Guide to Henry David Thoreau*, edited by William Cain, 153–80. New York: Oxford University Press, 2000.

Rueben, Paul. "American Transcendentalism: A Brief Introduction." Chapter 4 in *PAL: Perspectives on American Literature: A Research and Reference Guide*. web.csustan.edu/ english/reuben/pal/chap4/4intro.html (accessed May 13, 2002).

———. "Romanticism—A Brief Introduction." Chapter 3 in *PAL: Perspectives on American Literature: A Research and Reference Guide*. web.csustan.edu/english/reuben/ pal/chap3/3intro.html (accessed May 13, 2002).

Salt, Henry. "Gandhi and Thoreau." *Nation and Athenaeum* 46, no. 22 (1930): 728.

———. *The Life of Henry David Thoreau*. Hamden, CT: Archon Books, 1968.

Sayre, Robert. *Thoreau and the American Indians*. Princeton, NJ: Princeton University Press, 1977.

Schneider, Richard, ed. *Thoreau's Sense of Place: Essays in American Environmental Writing*. Iowa City: University of Iowa Press, 2000.

Schwartz, Barry. *The Paradox of Choice: Why More Is Less*. New York: Harper Perennial, 2005.

Tauber, Alfred. *Henry David Thoreau and the Moral Agency of Knowing*. Berkeley and Los Angeles: University of California Press, 2001.

Thoreau, Henry David. *The Annotated Walden*. Edited by Phillip Van Doren. New York: Clarkson N. Potter, 1970.

———. "Autumnal Tints." In *The Natural History Essays*, edited by Robert Sattelmeyer. Salt Lake City, UT: Peregrine Smith, 1980.

———. "Cape Cod." In *Walden and Other Writings by Henry David Thoreau*, edited by Joseph Wood Krutch, 407–18. New York: Bantam, 1981.

———. "Civil Disobedience." In *The Portable Thoreau*, rev. ed., edited by Carl Bode, 109–37. New York: Penguin, 1987.

———. "The Dispersion of Seeds." In *Faith in a Seed: The Dispersion of Seeds and Other Late Natural History Writings*, edited by Bradley Dean, 23–176. Washington, DC: Island Press, 1993.

———. *Excursions*. Edited by Bradford Torrey and Francis Allen. Boston: Houghton Mifflin, 1906.

———. *Faith in a Seed: The Dispersion of Seeds and Other Late Natural History Writings*. Edited by Bradley Dean. Washington, DC: Island Press, 1993.

———. "Huckleberries." In *The Natural History Essays*, edited by Robert Sattelmeyer, 211–62. Salt Lake City, UT: Peregrine Smith, 1980.

———. *Journal 1: 1837–1844*. Edited by Elizabeth Hall Witherall. Princeton, NJ: Princeton University Press, 1981.

———. *Journal 2: 1842–1848*. Edited by Robert Sattelmeyer. Princeton, NJ: Princeton University Press, 1984.

———. *Journal 3: 1848–1851*. Edited by Robert Sattelmeyer, Mark Patterson, and William Rossi. Princeton, NJ: Princeton University Press, 1990.

———. *Journal 4: 1851–1852*. Edited by Leonard Neufeldt and Nancy Craig Simmons. Princeton, NJ: Princeton University Press, 1992.

———. *Journal 5: 1852–1853*. Edited by Patrick O'Connell. Princeton, NJ: Princeton University Press, 1997.

———. *Journal 6: 1853*. Edited by William Rossi and Heather Kirk Thomas. Princeton, NJ: Princeton University Press, 2000.

———. *The Journal of Henry David Thoreau*. 14 vols. Edited by Bradford Torrey and Francis Allen. Boston: Houghton Mifflin, 1906.

———. *The Journal of Henry David Thoreau*. Salt Lake City, UT: Peregrine Smith, 1951.

———. *The Journal of Henry David Thoreau*. New York: Dover, 1962.

———. "The Last Days of John Brown." In *Reform Papers: The Writings of Henry D. Thoreau*, edited by Wendell Glick, 145–54. Princeton, NJ: Princeton University Press, 1973.

———. "Life without Principle." In *The Portable Thoreau*, rev. ed, edited by Carl Bode, 631–55. New York: Penguin, 1987.

———. *The Maine Woods*. Edited by Joseph Moldenhauer. Princeton, NJ: Princeton University Press, 1972.

———. *The Natural History Essays*. Edited by Robert Sattelmeyer. Salt Lake City, UT: Peregrine Smith, 1980.

———. "Paradise (to be) Regained." In *Reform Papers: The Writings of Henry D. Thoreau*, edited by Wendell Glick, 19–48. Princeton, NJ: Princeton University Press, 1973.

———. "A Plea for Captain John Brown." In *Reform Papers: The Writings of Henry D. Thoreau*, edited by Wendell Glick, 111–38. Princeton, NJ: Princeton University Press, 1973.

———. "Reform and Reformers." In *Reform Papers: The Writings of Henry D. Thoreau*, edited by Wendell Glick, 181–98. Princeton, NJ: Princeton University Press, 1973.

———. "The Service." In *Reform Papers: The Writings of Henry D. Thoreau*, edited by Wendell Glick, 3–18. Princeton, NJ: Princeton University Press, 1973.

———. "Slavery in Massachusetts." In *Reform Papers: The Writings of Henry D. Thoreau*, edited by Wendell Glick, 91–110. Princeton, NJ: Princeton University Press, 1973.

———. "Walden." In *The Portable Thoreau*, rev. ed., edited by Carl Bode, 258–572. New York: Penguin, 1987.

———. *Walden and Other Writings by Henry David Thoreau*. Edited by Joseph Wood Krutch. New York: Bantam, 1981.

———. "Walking." In *The Portable Thoreau*, rev. ed., edited by Carl Bode, 592–630. New York: Penguin, 1987.

———. *A Week on the Concord and Merrimack Rivers*. Edited by Carl F. Hovde, William Howarth, and Elizabeth Hall Witherell. Princeton, NJ: Princeton University Press, 1980.

———. "Wild Apples." In *Excursions*, edited by Bradford Torrey and Francis Allen, 253–91. Boston: Houghton Mifflin, 1906.

———. *Wild Fruits: Thoreau's Rediscovered Last Manuscript*. Edited by Bradley Dean. New York: W. W. Norton, 2000.

Timpe, Eugene, ed. *Thoreau Abroad: Twelve Bibliographical Essays*. Hamden, CT: The Shoestring Press, 1971.

Turner, Frederick. *Natural Classicism: Essays on Literature and Science*. New York: Paragon, 1985.

Van Doren Stern, ed. "Walden: The Book and Its Meaning." In *The Annotated Walden*. New York: Clarkson N. Potter, 1970.

Walker, Brian. "Thoreau's Alterative Economics: Work, Liberty, Democratic Cultivation." *American Political Science Review* 92, no. 4 (1998): 845–56.

Walls, Laura Dassow. "Introduction: The Man Most Alive." In *Material Faith: Henry David Thoreau on Science*, edited by Laura Walls and J. Parker Huber, ix–xviii. Boston: Mariner, 2001.

———. *Seeing New Worlds: Henry David Thoreau and Nineteenth-Century Natural Science*. Madison: University of Wisconsin Press, 1995.

Wilkes, Christopher. "A Modest Proposal Indeed." *Perspectives: Newsletter of the ASA Theory Section* 28, no. 3 (February 2006): 7–9.

Wilson, Leslie. "New England Transcendentalism." *Concord* (November 1998). www.concordma.com/magazine/nov98/trans.html (accessed May 14, 2002).

Witherell, Elizabeth, and Elizabeth Dubrulle. "The Life and Times of Henry D. Thoreau." In *The Writings of Henry D. Thoreau*. 1999. www.library.ucsb.edu/thoreau/thoreau_life.html (accessed June 27, 2000).

Worley, Sam MacGuire. *Emerson, Thoreau and the Role of the Cultural Critic*. Albany: State University of New York Press, 2001.

Yardley, Jonathan. "Ten Books That Shaped the American Character." *American Heritage* 24 (April/May 1985): 2–6.

Zeitlin, Irving. *Ideology and the Development of Sociological Theory*. 6th ed. Upper Saddle River, NJ: Prentice-Hall, 1997.

~

Index

"Resistance to Civil Government"
(Thoreau), 14. *See also* "Civil
Disobedience" (Thoreau)
Richardson, Robert D., Jr., 24, 88,
103–4
Riesman, David, 29
Ripley, George, 27
Ritzer, George, 4
Romanticism, 17, 19–20, 23–24, 33
Rousseau, Jean-Jacques, 19, 20, 21–22, 66

Salt, Henry, 29
Sanborn, F. B., 27
Satori, 102
"Satyagraha," 30
"sauntering," 116–17
"savage" society, vs. "civilization,"
66–69, 70, 71; as model, 70–71,
91n16, 91n19; simplicity of, 71; in
Spencer's vs. Thoreau's thought,
73–74
Sayre, Robert, 104
Schneider, Richard, 46
science, early naturalists compared to,
80–81; Enlightenment and, 18;
institutionalization of, 16;
interdisciplinary approach to, 81–82,
94n58; language of, 78, 79; as
sociological paradigm, 5, 6;
subjective approach to, 80–81,
93n48, 94n57; Thoreau's interest in,
17, 18, 24–26, 77; Thoreau's work
in, 25, 77, 90n1; as way of knowing,
77–80, 92n41, 93n 48, 93n50,
94n63. *See also* technology
scientific knowledge, critique of, 77–80,
92n41, 93n 48, 93n50, 94n63
scientific measurement, 77, 92n35
scientific observation, 79, 94n62,
116–17
seeing, "new ways of," 6, 100–2
self-cultivation, cycle of greed as threat
to, 69–70; defense of slavery as

threat to, 84–85; "savage" society's
lessons on, 70–72; self-examination
and, 21; self-reliance and, 24; and
social reform, 83
self-examination, 17, 21, 24; and
alienation, 50; in Transcendentalism,
18–19
self-reflective habits, 116–17
self-reform, 83, 95n71
self-reliance, 24; critiques of, 87, 89
sexism, in sociology, 5
shelter, 66–67, 67–68
Simmel, Georg, 113
simple living, 24, 65, 71, 87
Skinner, B. F., 29
slavery, citizen complacency toward, 56,
62n84, 62n86; government defense
of, 54–55, 84–85; as threat to
individual, 23, 84–85
"Slavery in Massachusetts," 14, 21; on
citizen complacency, 62n84; on
government, 50–51, 54–55; on
return of fugitive slaves, 96n79; on
social action, 84
Smith, Adam, 17, 24
social action, in Marx's thought, 49;
and sociology, 2, 5, 10; in Thoreau's
thought, 82–86; by
Transcendentalists, 19. *See also* social
reform
social analysis, by Thoreau: criticisms
of, 87–90; Durkheim's compared to,
74–75; Marx's compared to, 47–50;
Spencer's compared to, 73–74
social change, 65, 66, 82–86; means of
achieving, 82–86; in nineteenth
century, 15–17; in Rousseau's
thought, 20. *See also* social
evolution; social reform
social class, 41; in "civilized" vs.
"savage" society, 68–69; and
clothing, 41, 59n19; Thoreau's
explorations of, 105–6

About the Author

Shawn Chandler Bingham is an assistant professor of sociology at Saint Leo University in Saint Leo, Florida. He has served as a research fellow at the Center for Health and Disability Research at the National Rehabilitation Hospital in Washington, D.C. and has taught at several other colleges and universities. His primary research interests revolve around examining commonalities among the arts, humanities, and social sciences.